THE WAY PEOPLE LIVE

Life on a Medieval Pilgrimage

Titles in The Way People Live series include:
Cowboys in the Old West
Life During the French Revolution
Life in an Eskimo Village
Life in Ancient Greece
Life in the Warsaw Ghetto
Life in War-Torn Bosnia
Life on a Medieval Pilgrimage
Life on an Israeli Kibbutz

Life on a Medieval Pilgrimage

by Don Nardo

Lucent Books, P.O. Box 289011, San Diego, CA 92198-9011

Library of Congress Cataloging-in-Publication Data

Nardo, Don, 1947-
    Life on a medieval pilgrimage / Don Nardo.
      p.   cm. — (The way people live)
    Includes bibliographical references and index.
    Summary: Describes the daily life of pilgrims in the Middle Ages,
analyzing why they went on pilgrimages and what they hoped to accomplish.
    ISBN 1-56006-325-4 (alk. paper)
    1. Christian pilgrims and pilgrimages—History—Juvenile literature.
2. Travel, Medieval—Juvenile literature.   3. Civilization, Medieval—Juvenile
literature.   [1. Pilgrims and pilgrimages.   2. Religious life.   3. Middle
Ages.   4. Civilization, Medieval.] I. Title. II. Series.
  BX2323.S74   1996
   248.4'63'0902—dc20   95-20488
                                                CIP
                                                AC

Contents

FOREWORD
Discovering the Humanity in Us All   6

INTRODUCTION
A Civilization Obsessed with God   8

CHAPTER ONE
The City of God: How Faith Shaped and
Inspired the Medieval Mind   11

CHAPTER TWO
To See What Lay Beyond the Horizon:
The Pilgrims and Their Motives   23

CHAPTER THREE
"How Far Is It from Here to Paris?"
The Rules of a Successful Pilgrimage   34

CHAPTER FOUR
Medieval Mishaps and Mayhem:
When Pilgrimages Went Wrong   43

CHAPTER FIVE
Reaching a Spiritual Goal: Europe's Many
Sacred Shrines and Relics   53

CHAPTER SIX
The Ultimate Pilgrimage: Journey to
Jerusalem, the Furnace of God   65

CONCLUSION
A Modern March Through History   76

Notes   81
For Further Reading   85
Works Consulted   87
Additional Works Consulted   89
Index   91
Picture Credits   93
About the Author   95

Discovering the Humanity in Us All

The Way People Live series focuses on pockets of human culture. Some of these are current cultures, like the Eskimos of the Arctic; others no longer exist, such as the Jewish ghetto in Warsaw during World War II. What many of these cultural pockets share, however, is the fact that they have been viewed before, but not completely understood.

To really understand any culture, it is necessary to strip the mind of the common notions we hold about groups of people. These stereotypes are the archenemies of learning. It does not even matter whether the stereotypes are positive or negative; they are confining and tight. Removing them is a challenge that's not easily met, as anyone who has ever tried it will admit. Ideas that do not fit into the templates we create are unwelcome visitors—ones we would prefer remain quietly in a corner or forgotten room.

The cowboy of the Old West is a good example of such confining roles. The cowboy was courageous, yet soft-spoken. His time (it is always a he, in our template) was spent alternatively saving a rancher's daughter from certain death on a runaway stagecoach, or shooting it out with rustlers. At times, of course, he was likely to get a little crazy in town after a trail drive, but for the most part, he was the epitome of inner strength. It is disconcerting to find out that the cowboy is human, even a bit childish. Can it really be true that cowboys would line up to help the cook on the trail drive grind coffee, just hoping he would give them a little stick of pep-permint candy that came with the coffee shipment? The idea of tough cowboys vying with one another to help "Coosie" (as they called their cooks) for a bit of candy seems silly and out of place.

So is the vision of Eskimos playing video games and watching MTV, living in prefab housing in the Arctic. It just does not fit with what "Eskimo" means. We are far more comfortable with snow igloos and whale blubber, harpoons and kayaks.

Although the cultures dealt with in Lucent's The Way People Live series are often historically and socially well known, the emphasis is on the personal aspects of life. Groups of people, while unquestionably affected by their politics and their governmental structures, are more than those institutions. How do people in a particular time and place educate their children? What do they eat? And how do they build their houses? What kinds of work do they do? What kinds of games do they enjoy? The answers to these questions bring these cultures to life. People's lives are revealed in the particulars and only by knowing the particulars can we understand these cultures' will to survive and their moments of weakness and greatness.

This is not to say that understanding politics does not help to understand a culture. There is no question that the Warsaw ghetto, for example, was a culture that was brought about by the politics and social ideas of Adolf Hitler and the Third Reich. But the Jews who were crowded together in the ghetto cannot be understood by the Reich's politics. Their life was a day-to-day battle for existence, and the creativity and methods they used to prolong their lives is a vital story of human perseverance that would be denied by focusing only on the institutions of Hitler's Germany. Knowing that children as young as five or six outwitted Nazi guards on a daily basis, that Jewish policemen helped the Germans control the ghetto, that children attended secret schools in the ghetto and even earned diplomas—these are the things that reveal the fabric of life, that can inspire, intrigue, and amaze.

Books in the The Way People Live series allow both the casual reader and the student to see humans as victims, heroes, and onlookers. And although humans act in ways that can fill us with feelings of sorrow and revulsion, it is important to remember that "hero," "predator," and "victim" are dangerous terms. Heaping undue pity or praise on people reduces them to objects, and strips them of their humanity.

Seeing the Jews of Warsaw only as victims is to deny their humanity. Seeing them only as they appear in surviving photos, staring at the camera with infinite sadness, is limiting, both to them and to those who want to understand them. To an object of pity, the only appropriate response becomes "Those poor creatures!" and that reduces both the quality of their struggle and the depth of their despair. No one is served by such two-dimensional views of people and their cultures.

With this in mind, the The Way People Live series strives to flesh out the traditional, two-dimensional views of people in various cultures and historical circumstances. Using a wide variety of primary quotations—the words not only of the politicians and government leaders, but of the real people whose lives are being examined—each book in the series attempts to show an honest and complete picture of a culture removed from our own by time or space.

By examining cultures in this way, the reader will notice not only the glaring differences from his or her own culture, but also will be struck by the similarities. For indeed, people share common needs—warmth, good company, stability, and affirmation from others. Ultimately, seeing how people really live, or have lived can only enrich our understanding of ourselves.

A Civilization Obsessed with God

O n November 10, 1387, in the twentieth year of his reign, the English king Richard II made a pilgrimage to the shrine of Saint Edward in London's most renowned church, Westminster Abbey. According to the medieval chronicler Ranulf Higden, the king

> entered the city of London on the tenth day of November; and the mayor and the rest of the citizens of the said city, clad all of one suit of white and red, went forth to meet him with ceremony and rode in procession before him. . . . [At Westminster] the abbot [head priest] and convent of [the] monastery also came to meet him in solemn manner in their copes [formal priests' robes], as far as the King's Gate, and brought him upon carpets laid before him from that place to the church. And when he made his devotions [prayers] in the customary fashion, he withdrew to his palace.[1]

Such pilgrimages, or journeys made to view and pray at holy shrines, were quite common at the time, not only for lordly monarchs like Richard II, but also for common people from all walks of life. Usually, at these shrines the pilgrims gaped in awe at and tried to touch holy relics. These artifacts connected with famous holy men and women and important past religious events ranged from splinters of wood said to be taken from the cross Jesus had been crucified on to the arm bone or tooth of a particular saint.

Because Richard had come to London from a neighboring town, his pilgrimage was short and relatively safe. By contrast, many other pilgrimages in his day were considerably longer and more dangerous. For example, pilgrims traveling toward Rome from England and other northern European lands had to cross the towering and often treacherous Alps that spanned extreme northern Italy. A Spanish pilgrim, Pero Tafur, left behind this description of part of his journey through an Alpine pass in 1437:

> The next day I . . . arrived at the foot of the St. Gothard Pass, high up in the Alps. . . . It was now the end of August and the snow was melting in the heat, making the crossing extremely perilous. . . . Before entering the narrow defiles [small steep-walled valleys] firearms are discharged to bring down any loose snow from above, for such avalanches sometimes bury travelers.[2]

Many other dangers lurked to hinder the pilgrims in their holy journeys. Some, such as witches, werewolves (creatures half-man and half-wolf), and trolls (monstrous dwarves), which many people at the time believed inhabited remote forests, were only imaginary. But other perils were quite real, including wolves of the four-legged rather than two-legged variety, as well as tough and disreputable highwaymen. According to historian William Manchester:

This early sixteenth-century drawing depicts a religious pilgrim being taunted by Satan or one of his demons.

found in what at first seems an unlikely place—people's dreams. In medieval times, certain types of dreams were very common, one of which scholars Clara Winston and Richard Winston here describe:

> A dream is reported in which a dead child appears to its mother and shows a wet shroud. It begs the mother not to weep any longer, so that the shroud may dry. This dream is recorded in a number of variations—a dead child appears in one dream as a full-grown man, but afflicted with a limp. When the mother asks why he is limping, the dream figure brings forth a watering can from beneath his cloak and says it is full of the tears the mother has shed all these years, and he is condemned to carry the heavy thing around. The mother hastily promises that she will weep no more but devote herself to good works.[4]

God-centered Lives

Such dreams symbolized an idea very prevalent in medieval times, that death brought a person to a much better kingdom than the one he or she had inhabited on earth. According to this view, because the deceased person was with God, it was ultimately unnecessary for the living to worry or to mourn for that person. Many people did mourn, of course, but neither as deeply nor for as long as is common today, for the average person then was thoroughly resigned to the concept of death as inevitable and, at least for the righteous individual, beneficial.

This reveals a level of piety and blind faith that is difficult for most people today to comprehend. "Human beings had always been interested in God," comments noted

They were pitiless thieves, kidnappers, and killers, and they flourished because they were so seldom pursued. Between towns the traveler was on his own. . . . Sometimes these brigands traveled in roving gangs, waiting to ambush strangers; sometimes they stood by the road disguised as beggars or pilgrims, knives at the ready. . . . Therefore honest travelers carried well-honed daggers, knowing that they might have to kill and hoping they would have the stomach for it.[3]

Considering these and a host of other very real dangers, why did so many pilgrims routinely risk life and limb to visit faraway shrines when they could easily have stayed at home and worshiped at their local churches? A hint at the answer to this question can be

A band of pilgrims stops to rest at a local shrine on the way to the Holy Land in Palestine, the most sacred destination of medieval pilgrims.

scholar Charles Van Doren. But medieval people, he explains, tended to take that interest to an extreme:

> It can almost be said that they became obsessed with God. They thought about God, they studied God, they tried to ascertain his will and to obey it, and they tried to discover God's purposes in the world and to advance them. Their lives became more God-centered than ever before in Western history.[5]

Thus, in the medieval mind, simply attending one's local church was often not enough to

satisfy the driving urge to glorify and attain the closest possible contact with God. Pilgrimages to distant and exotic shrines offered compelling new opportunities for such blessed contact.

In view of this spiritual obsession, it is difficult to appreciate the seriousness and importance that medieval people placed on holy pilgrimages without first understanding the tight hold the Christian Church had on their lives and minds. Therefore, this examination of these spiritual journeys begins with a look at how the church came to shape and to dominate Europe and its inhabitants during one of history's most fascinating eras.

The City of God: How Faith Shaped and Inspired the Medieval Mind

The term "medieval" evolved from the Latin phrase *medium aevum*, meaning "the age in the middle." As near as historians can tell, the second-century Christian writer Tertullian coined the phrase in an attempt to place his own times in perspective. He grew up in a particularly peaceful and prosperous era when most of Europe was part of the Roman Empire. And he recognized that Roman civilization, with its broad and largely fair system of laws, its vast network of paved roads, and its concise yet highly descriptive Latin language, had unified and significantly benefited the more than 100 million people living in the lands ringing the Mediterranean Sea.

However, in Tertullian's day most Romans were pagans, or non-Christians. Being an extremely devout Christian, he believed that the pagan world, in spite of its good points, would eventually give way to one in which everyone accepted and lived by the creed set forth in the Christian Gospels, the texts that made up the biblical New Testament. In his view, then, he lived in an age midway between the traditional world of the Romans, Greeks, and other ancient peoples and the Christian world to come. Later historians appropriated Tertullian's term, the "middle ages," and applied it, along with the term "medieval," to the era falling between the ancient world and modern times. The era of the Middle Ages is usually dated from the mid–fifth century to the mid–fifteenth century—a span of about a millennium, or a thousand years.

Life in medieval times was very different from life today. Overall it was an age of superstition, in which most people believed in witches, demons, and omens, or supernatural signs of important impending events. It was an age of knights in armor who fought on horseback with lances, maces, and huge broadswords. It was also an era of extremes: Magnificent art, architecture, poetry, and music coexisted with horrifying tortures and constant brutal warfare; great intellectual writings were produced at a time when most people could neither read nor write; and a vast gulf existed between a handful of wealthy nobles and multitudes of poor peasants.

But most significantly, the medieval age was one of deep religious faith in which the Christian Church dominated all aspects of life. As medieval scholar Anne Fremantle explains:

> All over Europe there was one Church only. If a man were not baptized into it, he was not a member of society. Anyone excommunicated [denied salvation and damned to hell] by the Church lost his political and legal rights as well. . . . It was the Church that insisted that the poor did not have to fast as much as the rich, and which forbade servile work on Sunday. It was the Church which provided the poor

A congregation of clergymen carrying holy images, including crosses and hand-made copies of the scriptures, march in procession before a local ruler.

with social services—free food and hospitalization. There was, for a long while, no other source of education.[6]

A major reason that the church exerted so strong a grip on society was that it had managed to survive and actually to gain strength from what was probably the most decisive political and social upheaval in human history. This monumental event was the fall of Rome and the end of the unity Roman rule had brought to Europe. In a way, Tertullian's dream of a new Christian world replacing the old one came true, for the church filled the

vacuum left by Rome's demise and became a new unifying force for European civilization.

In the first three medieval centuries, many small, culturally backward kingdoms, inhabited by descendants of the tribes that had overrun Rome, dotted Europe. The leaders of these realms lacked the background, know-how, and will to maintain the remnants of Roman civilization, so many of the roads and bridges fell into disrepair, trade almost disappeared, and crude farming became the chief means of support for nearly everyone. The stark contrast between the old world and the new is revealed in European documents produced before and after Rome's demise. In the late second century, at Rome's height, Tertullian had written:

> Delightful farms have now blotted out every trace of the dreadful wastes; cultivated fields have supplanted woods; flocks and herds have driven out wild beasts . . . bogs have been drained. Large towns now occupy land hardly tenanted before by cottages. Thick population meets the eye on all sides. We overcrowd the world.[7]

In comparison, in the dismal sixth century, a Welsh monk and chronicler named Gildas complained that "every colony is leveled to the ground. The inhabitants are slaughtered and the flames crackled around. How horrible to behold the tops of towers torn from their lofty hinges, the stones of high walls, holy altars, mutilated corpses, all covered with lurid clots of blood as if they had been crushed together in some ghastly wine press."[8] And the eighth-century writer known as Paul the Deacon added:

> The flocks remained alone in the pastures. You see villas or fortified places filled with people in utter silence. The whole world seems brought back to its ancient stillness: no voice in the field, no whistling of shepherds. The harvests are untouched. Human habitations became the abodes of wild beasts.[9]

Rome's Cultural Leftovers

Because of the breakdown of the old organized society, little centralized authority existed in early medieval times. So, for fellowship

The Huns, a nomadic people who originated in central Asia, swept into Europe in the late fourth century, driving other tribal peoples, the so-called "barbarians," up to and over Rome's borders and thereby setting in motion the events that culminated in the collapse of the mighty Roman Empire.

The City of God: How Faith Shaped and Inspired the Medieval Mind **13** and mutual protection people tended to huddle together in small villages and on farms that supported extended families that included aunts, uncles, cousins, and in-laws. Earning a meager living and often barely managing to fend off starvation, the vast majority of the population had no time for learning, reading, or cultural pursuits. Life became very localized and insular, or narrow and confined. People mostly married and associated with fellow villagers and rarely communicated with the inhabitants of neighboring regions, with the result that often dialects of the same language spoken only thirty or forty miles away were difficult to understand.

In these localized areas, some vestiges of Rome's culture survived even though its structure as a nation and an empire was gone. As famed historian Henri Pirenne points out:

In the midst of the troubles, the insecurity, the misery and the anarchy which accompanied the [barbarian] invasions there was naturally . . . decline, but even in that decline there was preserved a physiognomy [group of characteristics] still distinctly Roman. The Germanic tribes were unable . . . to do without it. They barbarized it, but they did not consciously Germanize it.[10]

Among these cultural leftovers were the Latin language, which had already begun to combine with barbarian tongues, and certain basic concepts of law and justice. But by far the most visible and important of the surviving Roman institutions was the Christian Church. In fact, once exposed to Christian lore and ideas, Rome's largely pagan destroyers converted to the faith with extraordinary quickness, and Europe's obsession with God began.

A major reason for these mass conversions was the breakdown of Roman authority and society, which convinced most people that God had punished Rome for centuries of arrogance, corruption, and paganism. This

Be Ashamed, You Romans!

During the terrors of the barbarian invasions, many Roman Christians believed that the turmoil was a punishment sent by God for the sins committed by the inhabitants of Rome's empire. In his essay On the Government of God *(quoted in Norman Cantor's* The Medieval World: 300–1300*), the fifth-century Christian theologian Salvian expressed this view.*

"What hope, I ask you, can there be for the Roman state when barbarians are more chaste and pure than the Romans? . . . If my human frailty permitted, I should wish to shout beyond my strength, to make my voice ring through the whole world: Be ashamed, you Roman people everywhere, be ashamed of the lives you lead. No cities are free of evil haunts, no cities anywhere are free from indecency, except those in which barbarians have begun to live. Do we then wonder that we are wretched who are so impure, that we are conquered by the enemy who are outdone by them in honor, that they possess our properties who renounce our wickedness? It is neither the natural strength of their bodies that makes them conquer nor the weakness of our nature that makes us subject to defeat. Let no one think or persuade himself otherwise—it is our vicious lives alone that have conquered us."

idea was defined and preached forcefully by Aurelius Augustinus, later known as Saint Augustine, in his book *The City of God*, the first great literary work to shape the medieval mind. Augustine was born in 354 in a Roman town in northern Africa and as a young man aspired to a career as a government administrator. But in 387 he converted to Christianity and became first a priest and then the bishop of the northern African town of Hippo.

Embracing an Invisible Kingdom

When the Goths sacked Rome in 410, many distraught Romans claimed that the old pagan gods had punished Rome for turning to Christianity. Augustine's *The City of God* was intended as a response to this accusation. He insisted that the exact opposite had occurred—that the Christian God had punished and would continue to punish Rome for its many prior centuries of paganism and its continuing political corruption. Augustine then went on to suggest that worldly empires like Rome, which were mostly concerned with power, money, and other material rewards, could not and would not survive: Only by taking a more spiritual path, by fully embracing God and living strictly by his rules, could humanity find the ultimate reward, salvation. Augustine symbolized the battle between the material and spiritual worlds by postulating the existence of two cities, the *civitas terrena*, or earthly city, and the *civitas Dei*, the city of God: "Humanity is divided into two sorts: such as live according to man, and such as live according to God. These we mystically call the 'two cities' or societies, the one predestined to reign eternally with God, the other condemned to perpetual torment with Satan."[11]

Saint Augustine, whose writings and ideas profoundly inspired medieval churchmen and laymen alike.

Augustine's teachings were widely influential. Many people, including the descendants of those who had sacked Rome, came to see the collapse of the old world as divinely inspired and heeded the lesson seemingly embodied in that huge event. God, they reasoned, had wiped away the old pagan world for its sins and the inhabitants of the new post-Roman age must not repeat the mistakes of the past. And so, most early medieval Europeans rejected the old world, allowed its ruins to continue crumbling, and focused their efforts on building a society supported by spiritual rather than worldly values. In a sense, the European mind, once open and outward looking, turned inward to contemplate and embrace an invisible kingdom.

Feudal Loyalties

One of the strongest and most important tenets of this new religious doctrine that so strove for the godly rather than the earthly city was loyalty to a higher authority. Society, having become fragmented and in a sense having lost its way, sought someone or something to give it wholeness and direction. God,

of course, was the most obvious and most powerful manifestation of that higher authority.

But such authority also took on human dimensions in the form of kings and noble lords. Europe had broken down into a patchwork of petty kingdoms that had little if any centralized leadership. As society became increasingly localized in character, its basic unit became the manor, or country estate, consisting of a central manor house, usually a castle with high walls and a moat for protection against attackers; and the surrounding houses, villages, and farmlands that supported the lord of the manor. Such lords, especially those who wanted to expand their power and influence, needed loyal soldiers and followers to support them. These supporters, called retainers or vassals, wanted something in return for their service. This relationship

An English Country Manor

The great contrast between rich and poor in the Middle Ages is evident from a comparison between the homes of the peasants and the nobles. Most peasants lived in tiny shacks with thatched roofs and dirt floors, while their lords dwelled in magnificent stone manor houses. This 1397 description of an English nobleman's country manor comes from the Miscellaneous Inquisition *(quoted in Edith Rickert's* Chaucer's World*), a surviving local public record of the period.*

"Extent of the manor of Keevil in the county of Wiltshire, which was [the property] of the Earl of Arundel: Within that manor are a certain hall, a chief chamber, and a little chamber next [to it] with a certain latrine [toilet room] at the back of the same hall,

roofed with tiles. Item, a certain chamber below the said great chamber with a certain other chamber and latrine next [to it]. Item, a certain chapel and a cellar below the chapel. Item, a certain chamber called "le warderobe" likewise at the end of the hall, and the entrance thereof is a certain great chamber with a latrine, and below that chamber is a certain pantry and buttery [place where butter was churned]. Item, there is a great kitchen newly repaired. . . . Item, a certain chamber beyond the gate with a latrine, entirely roofed with tiles. Item . . . a certain long stable and a certain little stable and a certain barn . . . but is in great need of repair. Item, there is . . . a certain dovecote [pigeon house] and two gardens."

Charles Martel, whose forces turned back the Muslims at Tours, France, in the eighth century, an event that helped solidify Christianity in Europe.

was the basis of the medieval feudal system. The Winstons explain:

> The vassal "commended" himself to his lord in the ceremony of homage, placing his hands in the lord's hands and swearing fealty [loyalty]. Essentially a pact was made, with the vassal undertaking certain fixed obligations, especially to defend the lord with his body. In return the lord promised protection and economic maintenance. . . . When the lord was an important chieftain, he had great lands to give away to his comrades in arms. . . . [The vassals], in their turn, had far more land than they could properly exploit or hold. . . . They could distribute the land among others who in their turn were subvassals. Periodically the lord sent word to his vassals, reminding them of their duty to him. They in turn rallied their men, each of whom brought their dependents . . . for counsel, training or warfare.[12]

Thus, a social hierarchy, a ladder with steps of increasing authority, developed. A lord had his vassals, who in turn had their own, and the lord himself was vassal to the most powerful and respected lord of all—the local king. Such kings were not all-powerful monarchs because their authority rested on the allegiance of their vassals, who could and sometimes did gang up to make kings do their bidding. These kings, vassals, and subvassals became Europe's landed nobility, the system of princes, dukes, earls, counts, and barons that endured for centuries and, at least in name, still exists today.

The Church as a Unifying Force

The result of the feudal exchange of land for service, particularly military service, was that most vassals became highly trained and efficient fighters, or knights, most of whom fought mounted on horses. The powerful potential of these mounted knights became apparent after the Battle of Tours in west-central France in 732. There, led by the powerful French lord Charles Martel, a force of Christian knights defeated an army of Muslims who had earlier crossed from northern Africa into Spain and were now bent on invading and colonizing the rest of Europe.

A serf delivers eggs, bread, and poultry to the steward of the local lord, part of the payment of indebtedness that lay at the heart of the medieval manorial system.

This victory seemed to validate the worth of the lord-vassal arrangement. After Martel rewarded his knights with grants of land, thereby creating thousands of new vassal manors, the feudal system became widespread and entrenched in Europe.

It is important to note that Martel recognized that the system could not work well without the church to back it up. The knights at Tours had fought not only to save their lands, but also to keep non-Christians, by now seen as a corrupt and polluting element, out of France. Martel and his immediate successors, including his grandson, the renowned king Charlemagne, saw that Christianity was a tremendous unifying force that could bind followers to a lord or king by giving them something glorious to fight for—the honor of God. Thus, religious faith, embodied in the church, and the feudal system united in a common effort to secure the loyalty of the common people, and in the process each institution drew strength from the other.

"Yes Indeed, It Is Very Hard Work"

In fact, the common people, who made up well over 90 percent of the population, were the vital underpinning that supported both the church and feudal lords. The church needed legions of the faithful to sustain and perpetuate itself and its message. At the same time the lords and their vassals required cheap laborers, since food had to be grown and manors maintained, and the nobles usually felt themselves above doing menial work. Consequently, another social order based on loyalty to a higher authority—called the manorial system because the manor was its central focus—evolved within the larger framework of feudalism.

In the manorial system, in exchange for a lord's protection a group of poor peasants became his serfs, agricultural laborers tied to his land and bound to serve him for life. Typically, a lord provided his serfs with from four to forty acres of land to farm, along with the rights to draw water from his springs and wells and to gather wood from his forests. In exchange, the serfs agreed to work a pre-scribed number of days on the lord's land or in his house and also to give him some of the crops they raised on their own land. Summarizing the mundane and often harsh lifestyle of the serfs, Anne Fremantle writes:

Only about 10 percent of medieval people lived in towns; most of the rest were peasants on manorial farms. The average peasant had a small holding of land, a rude home with thatched roof and dirt floor, and heavy obligations to render work and produce to his lord. His whole world—his village, the manorhouse, the surrounding fields and woods—might encompass less than two square miles. . . .

In this medieval woodcut, a peasant plows a field on a manor owned by a local lord. That manor and the farmlands and villages surrounding it probably constituted the peasant's whole world.

Each autumn the peasants sowed wheat and rye; each spring they planted other grains plus legumes; each summer they harvested both crops. Between these periods of back-breaking labor came many lesser chores.[13]

The seemingly unending toil the serfs endured, often for very minimal reward, is revealed in this dialogue between the early English writer Aelfric the Grammarian and a serf, reported in Aelfric's *Colloquium:*

"Well, plowman, how do you work?" "Oh, Sir, I work very hard. I go out at dawn,

A late fifteenth-century engraving, attributed to the noted artist Albrecht Dürer, depicts swarms of demons rising from the depths of hell to capture the souls of sinners.

driving the oxen to the field and I yoke them to the plow. . . . Every day I must plow a full acre or more. . . ." "Have you any mate [helper]?" "I have a boy, who drives the oxen. . . . He is now hoarse from cold and shouting [at the oxen]." "Well, is it very hard work?" "Yes indeed, it is very hard work."[14]

Occasionally, a very ambitious serf, working extra hours over the course of years, accumulated enough money and/or goods to buy freedom from the arrangement he had with his lord. But the majority of peasants, though they were not slaves, remained tied to their manors out of some combination of need, habit, fear of change, and loyalty.

The Church Struggles for Supremacy

Another reason the majority of serfs perpetuated the system was their steadfast devotion to the church and what they perceived as God's intended scheme. One common belief was that everyone had his or her allotted role or position in the social order and that God had ordained the serf's position to be lowly. According to this view, earthly status was relatively unimportant anyway because in the spiritual world thought to exist beyond the earthly one everyone, lord and serf alike, was equal and received salvation.

To instill and maintain such blind devotion from its followers, the church needed to exert as much control as possible over all levels of society. And to establish that control, church leaders, especially the pope, Christendom's highest earthly official, needed a significant say in how people ran their lives. Over the centuries, most popes strove toward the goal of theocracy, a system in which the

Saint Benedict lectures some of his followers. The Benedictine Order, whose members took strict vows of poverty, chastity, and obedience, inspired many other monastic orders in the Middle Ages.

church would have supreme authority over secular, or nonchurch, affairs, an authority greater even than that of the kings. But the kings and nobles, though themselves devout Christians who recognized the church's role in society, were reluctant to hand over their sovereignty completely to the clergy. Therefore, a long, on-and-off power struggle ensued between the popes and secular ruling classes.

The Clerical Hierarchy

The church was much more successful in controlling the masses of commoners who made up the bulk of its flock. But control was not an easy task, considering that the pope, though

powerful, lived in Rome, which seemed extremely remote in an age when most people rarely traveled even to their neighboring valley. First, playing on public fears, the church regularly emphasized that those who did not adhere strictly to the faith would be damned to hell. "Hell's torments were lovingly dwelt on and elaborated," comments medieval scholar Louise Collis. "Every kind of roasting, screwing [twisting metal screws into the flesh], beating, boiling, disemboweling [cutting out the internal organs], was described in words, paint, and sculpture." [15]

Second, the church maintained contact with and control over its flock through local clergymen, who, in the pope's stead, acted as mediators between humans and God. Two distinct branches of the clergy evolved: the priesthood, which provided ordinary people with religious ceremonies, sermons, Holy Communion, and sacraments such as baptism and marriage; and monastic, or monastery-dwelling, orders such as the Benedictines, founded by Saint Benedict of Nursia in the sixth century. These monks took vows of poverty, chastity, and obedience and spent most of their time praying and meditating in secluded monasteries. In general, the priests looked after people's everyday spiritual needs, while the monks set an example of holiness for others to follow and became missionaries spreading the faith to nonbelievers.

Through its clerical hierarchy, beginning with the priests and monks and ascending through the bishops and cardinals to the pope, the church maintained contact with its followers and helped to guide them through the trials and tribulations of their lives. In this way it held the fabric of medieval life together. And it also ensured its own survival by perpetuating the faith from one generation to the next.

A new bishop is consecrated. The bishops, each in charge of a geographical region and all the churches and local priests within it, were an important part of the church's hierarchy.

Answering a Divine Summons

The widespread belief that God called on the faithful to journey to the Holy Land (Jerusalem in Palestine, where Jesus is supposed to have lived and died) to pray is illustrated in the memoirs of a French clergyman, Abbot Guibert of Nogent. Guibert recalled the story of an English king who had been long pondering the meaning of life and the existence of God. As the story went, to the king's surprise God inspired him to go on a pilgrimage to the Holy Land, where his questions would be answered:

> God, Who declares better things to men of good will, sent a voice from heaven to urge the man to go to Jerusalem, where he would hear what ought to be believed about God, how the Son of God proceed-ed from God, and lived among men for their sake, what He [Christ] endured, what became of Him, and what vicars of his divine name he left behind as models. He [the king] was told that when he had gone there, the Mother [the Virgin Mary] and all the Apostles would explain these great mysteries to him.[16]

All through the Middle Ages, many European men and women heard the same kind of otherworldly voice, believing it to be a divine summons emanating from what Augustine had called the City of God. Out of awe, reverence, fear, and guilt, they were driven to answer this summons and embark on holy pilgrimage. For in their hearts they were convinced that this demonstration of their faith would ensure that one day they would reach and enter the gates of that glorious city.

To See What Lay Beyond the Horizon: The Pilgrims and Their Motives

Medieval religious pilgrims represented a broad cross section of society, ranging from kings and nobles to priests and monks, and from merchants and doctors to ordinary workaday peasants. Yet because long journeys were not cheap, only certain segments of society could afford to go on pilgrimage often or at any time they chose. Sufficient funds were required for inns and other accommodations along the way, fees for ship passage, tolls, guidebooks, and numerous other expenses. Poor people had to save their pennies for many years to pay for a single trip, but they considered the effort well worth it, for a pilgrimage was, almost without exception, the highlight of their lives. Even so, a majority of the poor never were able to scrape together the necessary funds, which meant that most of the pilgrims seen along the roadways tended to be members of the middle and upper classes.

Pilgrims embarked on their religious odysseys for a wide variety of reasons. The most obvious and perhaps most common was the desire to witness firsthand the places where famous Christian figures, such as Jesus Christ, the Virgin Mary, and various saints from all across Europe had lived, preached, and/or died. Seeing and touching relics associated with such holy personages was held to be a blessed and uplifting experience. Other motivations for going on pilgrimage included seeking pardon and relieving guilt for one's

Geoffrey Chaucer, the English writer whose work, The Canterbury Tales, *contains many revealing insights about medieval people and customs.*

sins, doing penance after committing a crime, and looking for adventure in faraway and exotic locales.

Chaucer's Pilgrims

No surviving medieval document captures the range of motives for going on a pilgrimage better than Geoffrey Chaucer's *The Canterbury Tales*. Chaucer, born about 1340, was an En-

Canterbury Cathedral, the ultimate destination of Chaucer's pilgrims and today one of England's most renowned landmarks.

glish civil servant and diplomat who served a number of important kings and nobles in his career. As a sideline he wrote long poems, beginning his most famous, *The Canterbury Tales*, about 1387 and leaving it unfinished at his death in 1400. The work's more than seventeen thousand lines of verse and prose tell the tale of twenty-nine pilgrims who meet in the Tabard Inn in the town of Southwark, a suburb of London, at the start of a pilgrimage to the renowned cathedral at Canterbury, located some fifty miles to the southeast. Even though the work is fictional, Chaucer based his characters on real-life situations and individuals. Historians believe it to be an accurate account of such pilgrimages.

Chaucer did not bother to explain to his readers why the pilgrims wanted to go to Canterbury. At the time, Canterbury Cathedral housed the most famous and revered shrine in England and its contents and background were common knowledge. Everyone knew the story of King Henry II and his close friend and adviser Thomas Becket; how, in an attempt to check the growing power of the English bishops, in 1161 Henry made Becket archbishop of Canterbury, the highest religious post in the land; how, to Henry's surprise, Becket was so inspired by his new position that he renounced all luxury and put his duty to God before his duty to the king; and how four of Henry's knights, thinking they were doing the king a favor, murdered Becket in his own cathedral. Scholar Gertrude Hartman explains why this act made Becket a holy martyr and inspired generations of pilgrims:

> To kill anyone within the sacred precincts of the church was an unspeakable crime, and the news of Becket's death filled all Europe with horror. The people feared that the curse of God would fall on a land where such a terrible thing had been done. Becket became a holy martyr of the church, and a magnificent shrine was built for him in the cathedral where he had lost his life. . . . It was a frequent sight in the spring of the year to see bands of pilgrims making their way to Canterbury to the martyr's shrine. In the course of time these pilgrimages came to be looked upon as outings. There was always a sense of adventure in a journey to a new place in medieval times, and it gave people a chance to see the world.[17]

Thus, Chaucer's pilgrims, like pilgrims all over Europe, were driven by a combination of religious devotion and the urge to see what lay beyond the horizon of the small world of their home village or valley.

Serving God in Different Ways

The Canterbury Tales also reveals the various kinds of people that went on these religious journeys. Of the twenty-nine travelers that meet at the Tabard Inn, a relatively large proportion are members of the clergy or religious officials of one type or another. Chaucer lists three priests, and a monk and a

Chaucer's pilgrims, including a prioress, a pardoner, a parson, a monk, a friar, and three priests, leave the Tabard Inn to begin their journey to Canterbury.

friar, both of whom represent monastic or more specialized orders of clergy. They are accompanied by a nun and a prioress, or head nun at a priory, a convent where nuns lived and prayed. Also along on the trip is a parson, or priest who had charge of a poor country parish, and a pardoner, a church official whose task was, at the orders of a priest, to pardon people who had performed sufficient penance for their sins.

The fact that about one quarter of the party is affiliated in some way with the church indicates that clergy and church officials must have been among the most common kinds of pilgrims. It also suggests that the unusually strong sense of faith prevalent in medieval times drew a sizable percentage of the population to these religious ranks. No

accurate figure for that percentage has survived but it was undoubtedly much higher than it is now.

Though all of these church representatives served God in one way or another, their attitudes and methods were often very different, and one should not assume that they got along well with one another when traveling together on a pilgrimage. For example, rivalry and mutual contempt between priests and monks was not uncommon. Priests generally benefited greatly from the tithe, or church tax—usually consisting of 10 percent of a person's income—that all members of his parish had to pay. Priests also received fees for the various services they performed, and some dipped their hands into the pot containing funds collected for charity. Consequently, a

The pardoner, one of the colorful pilgrims in The Canterbury Tales. *His tale illustrates the sin of greed by describing three men who set out to avenge the death of a friend but instead find a treasure of gold along the way and, in the process of fighting over it, kill one another.*

Friars, like other pilgrims, made token personal sacrifices in their religious journeys. For some, having to cut off a beard when returning could be such a sacrifice. Most men let their beards grow while on pilgrimage but members of some religious orders, including the Dominicans, had to be clean shaven at all other times. In this surviving tract (quoted in Clara and Richard Winston's Daily Life in the Middle Ages*), a Dominican friar laments the loss of his whiskers.*

"Unwillingly, I must say, I had it [the beard] off, because it seemed to me that in it I looked bolder, more considerable, more robust, comely [handsome] and reverend, and if I might rightly have kept it, I would rather not have parted from it, as it is a natural ornament embellishing a man's face, and makes him appear strong and formidable."

sizable proportion of these priests, especially the bishops and other high officials, became financially well off and enjoyed luxuries comparable to those of many nobles. This often angered the monks, who saw the majority of priests as corrupt individuals, and inspired many monks to live in poverty and seclusion.

Strong disagreements and rivalries also existed between the monks and friars. In the early 1200s, Domingo de Guzmán, later Saint Dominic, who preached in Spain and southern France, and Francis of Assisi, later Saint Francis, who preached in Italy, both objected strongly to the idea of clergymen's withdrawing from the regular world. This, they said, clearly went against Christ's order to his disciples to go out into the world and urge people to repent and follow God. So Dominic

and Francis founded the Dominican and Franciscan orders of friars, respectively, whose members dedicated themselves to public service and extreme poverty. According to scholar J. J. Bagley:

> The friars stood out in startling contrast to the monks. Everyone could see they took their vows more seriously than the monks did. Instead of withdrawing into their cloisters [monasteries], they shared the trials of poverty with the meanest [poorest] beggars, and were always ready to earn their food by working in the fields and workshops. They did not demand

A fourteenth-century Franciscan friar contemplates a cross. The friars objected to monastic life and chose instead to live in poverty among the common people.

rents and tithes; at most they begged a few scraps of food when they had not been able to earn any, and some cast-off clothing when their rags would no longer hold together. Little wonder that the coming of the friars inspired a religious revival, that crowds flocked to hear them preach, and that many worthy men wished to forsake all and join them.[18]

Chaucer's description of the friar who goes on pilgrimage to Canterbury accurately reveals that these men, though highly devout, were not necessarily solemn or overly serious in their manners. This particular friar is "a wanton and a merry . . . a very festive man." Out of all the friars in the various orders, Chaucer wrote, there "is none that can equal his gossip and his fair language." He is "well liked by all and intimate [friendly] with franklins [small farmers] everywhere in his country, and with the worthy women of the town."[19]

Escape from Monotony

Chaucer's *Tales* illustrates still another interesting facet of the religious types who went on pilgrimages, namely that some did so against the wishes of their superiors in the church hierarchy. The fact that two nuns are in the group is particularly revealing. For centuries before Chaucer's time, church leaders had discouraged nuns from going on pilgrimage, issuing rules such as this one, published in 1195: "In order that the opportunity of wandering may be taken from nuns we forbid them to take the path of pilgrimage."[20] In 1318, only a few years before the journey Chaucer depicts, the archbishop of York forbade the nuns of an English convent to become pilgrims. The punishment he pre-

A Greedy Friar

Not all friars were as devoted to poverty and charity as they should have been. As is true of people in all walks of life, a few took advantage of others when they could, as evidenced in this excerpt from Mirour de l'omme, *or* Mirror of the Soul (*quoted in* Chaucer's World), *by John Gower, a fourteenth-century English poet who was a friend of Chaucer's. Here, Gower's friar goes to a poor couple's house, supposedly to comfort them, and ends up taking their last penny and eating all their food.*

Oh, how the friar behaves himself
When he comes to the house of a
    poor man!
Oh, well he knows how to preach!
Though the woman has little or
    nothing,
No less for that does he refrain
From claiming, praying, adjuring
    [overall, putting on a show of
    piety];
The half-penny he takes if there's no
    penny,
Even the only egg there is for
    supper—
He has to have something [to eat].
"Woe," says God, "upon the
    vagabond [bum]
Who comes thus to visit
The house that a poor woman keeps!"

scribed for those who defied the rule was to recite aloud one psalm, or sacred hymn, for each day the journey would have taken.

The attitudes and policies of male authority figures in the church regarding pilgrim nuns constituted a double standard. Yet the popes and archbishops who set these policies apparently felt that they were only acting in the nuns' best interests. They believed that some of the rough language and worldly images and ideas the nuns would encounter on these trips would shock them and perhaps do them lasting damage. One of Chaucer's more colorful pilgrims, the "wife of Bath," is the type of person church leaders most wanted the nuns to avoid—the low-bred secular woman who freely commits numerous small sins, largely gets away with them, and, most damaging of all, talks about them openly and unashamedly. The wife of Bath lives up to this stereotype when she argues loudly that, despite what prudes and fanatic religious types might say, the genitals were made for sex as well as urination:

Tell me also, to what purpose or end
The genitals were made, that I defend,
And for what benefit was man first wrought [made]?
Trust you right well, they were not made for naught [nothing]
[Regardless of those who] argue up and down
That they were made for passing out, as known,
Of urine, and our two belongings small [genitals]
Were just to tell a female from a male,
And for no other cause—ah, say you no?
Experience knows well it is not so.[21]

Chaucer's "wife of bath," whose story in The Canterbury Tales *is preceded by an 856-line prologue in which she describes her five late husbands and vigorously condemns the concept of celibacy.*

But this and other frank speeches by the wife of Bath do not shock Chaucer's prioress, nor in fact bother her in the least. In some ways the prioress, Madame Eglentyne, based on a real-life figure, is the typical medieval nun—reverent, clean, and neatly dressed, with perfect manners and a tender heart. "She was so charitable and piteous," Chaucer wrote, "that she would weep if she but saw a mouse caught in a trap, though it were dead or bled." [22] But she is forceful and daring enough to place the holy reasons for going on pilgrimage above the church's rules forbidding nuns these journeys. And having already gone on such trips, she has become worldly and knowledgeable enough about secular life that she surely finds the wife of Bath more charming and earthy than shocking and perverse.

In fact, for the prioress, going on pilgrimage is perhaps the only way to escape the confines of the convent, to see and at least to some degree to enjoy the world. After all, though she loves and worships God, she never really wanted to close herself up behind the convent's walls in the first place. That decision, one dictated by social custom, had been made for her and had condemned her to a secluded and largely boring life filled with repetition. As scholar Eileen Power explains:

> Eglentyne became a nun because her father did not want the trouble and expense of finding her a husband, and because being a nun was about the only career for a well-born lady who did not marry. Moreover, by this time [the fourteenth century], monks and nuns had grown more lazy, and did little work with their hands and still less with their heads, particularly in nunneries, where the early tradition of learning had died out and where many nuns could hardly under-

stand the Latin in which their services were written. The result was that the monastic life began to lose that essential variety which St. Benedict had designed for it, and as a result the regularity sometimes became irksome, and the series of services degenerated into a mere routine of peculiar monotony. [23]

The prioress takes advantage of the outlet of pilgrimage to escape this monotony; for her such journeys were, in effect, a mixture of business and pleasure. Nevertheless, she cannot go on pilgrimage alone, for even she recognizes the need for protection from thieves and other dangers that lurk along the way. So she takes along her "nun chaplain," a regular nun who assists her and acts as her daily companion, and three local priests who agree to go along on the trip.

Some Women Independent

The church fathers who discouraged nuns like Madame Eglentyne from going on pilgrimages in order to keep them away from crude secular women need not have worried. Few secular women went on these journeys. As the Winstons point out, both secular and church authorities frowned on the idea of women pilgrims because "the dangers of travel were considerable, and there seemed little likelihood that unaccompanied women could pass unmolested. Hence, pilgrimages for women were reserved for high-born ladies who could afford to bring with them a retinue of knights for their protection." [24]

Yet a few women of lesser means did go on pilgrimages, even long ones, alone. Some of these women braved the dangers because of their fanatical devotion to God, as was the case with Margery Kempe, a middle-class

Englishwoman who traveled alone to Jerusalem and other holy cities in the early 1400s. According to Louise Collis, who has studied and interpreted Kempe's memoirs, Margery was so devout that she sternly lectured almost everyone she met about the virtues of faith and the evils of sin and even believed that she herself had received blessed visions of Christ. In her lectures, writes Collis,

> She lingered over dreams of a martyr's death by fire, execution, drowning and hurricane. . . . These imaginings were particularly delightful since Christ himself had assured her that she would never come to harm at any man's hands. At the same time, he thanked her for her willingness to suffer for his sake. It showed the great merit of her soul, he said.[25]

Other women went alone on pilgrimage because they had unusually strong and independent personalities and were not afraid to defy male authority figures. Many medieval peasant women, for instance, were tough, earthy characters who dominated timid husbands and made most of the important family decisions. If they wanted to go on pilgrimage and could manage to raise the money (which was rare), they went, whether their husbands liked it or not.

Other Women Servile

By contrast, many (although not all) women of higher means or social status had husbands who were more well-to-do, more politically or socially powerful, and hence more dominating. Consequently, these women often tended to be less independent, more fearful of male authority, and more servile. For them, going on a pilgrimage was a way to escape the strict routine and in some cases the cruelty of married life, for wife beating was common and, because men wrote and enforced the laws, in some cases even legal. An influential thirteenth-century Dominican monk preached that "a man may chastise [punish] his wife and beat her for correction, for she is of the household, therefore the lord [husband] may chastise his own."[26] And when the new French town of Villefranche was established in the same century, one of its legal statutes declared: "All [male] inhabitants of Villefranche have the right to beat their wives, provided they do not kill them thereby."[27]

There were exceptions to this rule, of course. Some men adored their wives and treated them with gentleness, kindness, and respect. An outstanding example was Thomas Betson, a forty-year-old English merchant, who wrote to his fiancée (and cousin) in 1476:

> My own heartily beloved Cousin Katherine, I recommend me to you with all my heart. The token you sent is most welcome to me. Also a letter from your gentle squire telling me you are in good health and merry at heart. . . . By your faithful lover and Cousin, Thomas Betson, I send you this ring for a token [of my love].[28]

In any case, for fear of robbery, rape, or worse, women almost never traveled long distances alone. After Margery Kempe, bound for Venice, crossed the Alps accompanied only by William Weaver, a frail old man, she met up with a group of former traveling companions, who were astounded that she was alive and unhurt. According to Collis, "Only a miracle, they felt, could have brought her and feeble old Mr. Weaver safely over those terrible passes. . . . Perhaps [they suggested] she had traveled by supernatural means, flying through the air for instance."[29]

"He Loved God Most"

Like many pilgrims, Margery Kempe had more than one motive for her religious journeys. In addition to her extreme devotion to God, which gave her a burning desire to see famous holy shrines up close, she also became a pilgrim in hopes of receiving pardon for a "secret" and "horrible" former sin, the nature of which she never revealed in her memoirs. Like most other people of her day, she was convinced that going on pilgrimage would show God that she was sorry for her error and that he would excuse her and allow her into heaven.

Another common motive for pilgrimage was the widespread belief that such a journey, if made with enough sincerity and piety, could help cure illness, either that suffered by the pilgrim or by the pilgrim's loved one or friend. While on pilgrimage in the 1400s, Margaret Paston, a devout Englishwoman, wrote to her sick husband:

> Right worshipful husband, I recommend me to you, desiring to hear of your welfare, thanking God of the amending [healing] of the great disease that you have had. . . . I have promised to go on pilgrimage to Walsingham and to St. Leonard's Priory for you. I pray you, send me word as hastily as you may, how your sore [illness] doeth.[30]

Walsingham, located about one hundred miles northeast of London, was famous throughout Europe for its shrine built in 1061 to honor the Virgin Mary. Margaret and many others believed that the spirit of Christ's mother was particularly sympathetic to those struck by illness or disease.

Holy pilgrimage was also commonly used to punish and reform criminals, whose souls, it was thought, would be saved from hell by performing this act of repentance for their crimes. Often, the church, which had its own courts, stepped in and took over cases from the secular courts. Although church leaders believed wrongdoers should be punished, they also wanted to save as many souls as possible from damnation in hell, so they frequently ordered criminals to cleanse their blackened souls by going on long and very strict and arduous pilgrimages. Journeys lasting six, ten, or twelve years are documented, and, William Manchester adds:

> Offenders were ordered to shave their heads, abandon their families, fast constantly [usually eating only once a day], and set out barefoot for a far destination. Journey's end varied from offender to offender. Rome was a popular choice. Some were sent all the way to Jerusalem. The general rule was the longer the distance, the greater the atonement [divine pardon]. If of noble birth, the penitent had to wear chains on his neck and wrists forged from his own armor, a sign of how far he had fallen.[31]

Perhaps the most notorious of these criminal penitents was Count Fulk of Anjou, called "the Black." After twenty years of hideous crimes, including the murder of his own wife, Fulk received a sentence from a church court so severe that he supposedly fainted when he heard it. He had to make the long pilgrimage to Jerusalem and back three times, a total of over 15,300 miles, shackled in chains. On the last leg of the journey, monks tied him to a board and dragged him

"If Your Breath Is Bad, Hold It"

Medieval women of the middle and upper classes were expected to behave in a gentle, strict, and dignified manner at all times, particularly in public. This excerpt from Chatoiement des Dames, *a guide to proper female behavior by Robert of Blois, a poet of the period, is taken from Joseph and Frances Gies's* Life in a Medieval City.

"On the way to church or elsewhere, a lady must walk straight and not trot or run, or idle either. She must salute even the poor. She must let no one touch her on the breast except her husband. For that reason, she must not let anyone put a pin or a brooch on her bosom. No one should kiss her on the mouth except her husband. If she disobeys this injunction, neither loyalty, faith nor noble birth will avert the consequences. . . . If a man courts a lady, she must not boast of it. It is base [unseemly] to boast. . . . A lady does not accept gifts. For gifts which are given you in secret cost dear; one buys them with one's honor. . . . Women must not swear, drink too much or eat too much. . . . Ladies with pale complexions should dine early. Good wine colors the face. If your breath is bad, hold it in church when you receive the blessing. Cut your fingernails frequently, down to the quick, for cleanliness' sake. Cleanliness is better than beauty."

through the streets of Jerusalem while two men beat him brutally with bullwhips. Incredibly, Fulk survived this terrifying, years-long ordeal. Whether it saved his soul, of course, only God knows.

But people like Fulk were more the exception than the rule. Most pilgrims were ordinary God-fearing individuals who made these journeys out of simple but deep faith and devotion. They came from all walks of life, as in Chaucer's group, which includes: a knight who has fought in fifteen battles; the knight's trusty squire, who assists him in all endeavors; a miller with a red beard who loves to wrestle; a reeve, or town official; a franklin, or small landowner, who is particularly fond of wine; a manciple, or secular court officer; and also a cook, a clerk, a merchant, a sailor, a doctor, a lawyer, a carpenter, a weaver, and a common peasant plowman. The plowman's character perhaps best sums up why he and so many countless others in that era were so eager to go on pilgrimage. "Living in peace and perfect charity," Chaucer wrote, "he loved God most, and that with his whole heart and at all times."[32]

"How Far Is It from Here to Paris?" The Rules of a Successful Pilgrimage

In planning their trips, prospective pilgrims had many matters to consider and details to attend to. First, they had to get either permission or blessings from their local bishop. They also had to choose a convenient and safe route, one with sufficient accommodations for travelers; prepare their clothes; and find someone to look after their home and/or business while they were away. Luckily, as long as they had enough money saved for the trip itself, few travelers had to worry about falling into debt while away, for laws favoring and protecting pilgrims existed all across Europe. While on their religious journeys,

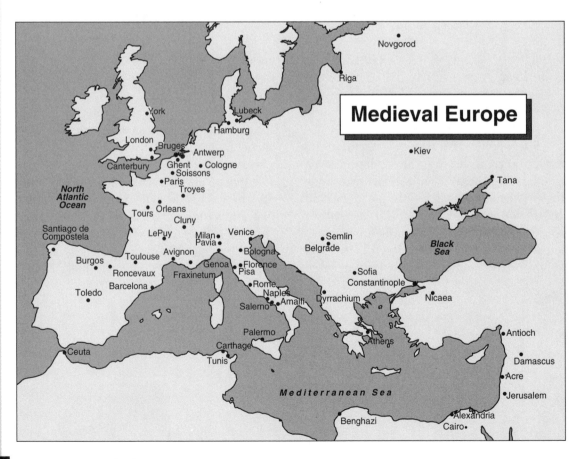

A group of villagers pay the tithe, or church tax, to their local priest. He was allowed to use the money to pay his way on a holy pilgrimage.

pilgrims were exempt from paying all taxes and no one could seize their land or belongings for any reason. A priest who went on pilgrimage could collect his whole year's stipend, the money he received from the local tithe, in one lump sum, which he could then use to finance the trip and for any other purposes he desired. Providing that a pilgrim followed the accepted rules of custom and that nothing unexpectedly went seriously wrong on the pilgrimage, he or she could look forward to a successful and spiritually enlightening journey.

The Initial Preparations

The first step in planning a pilgrimage, seeking permission, varied according to the trip. Usually, permission was not required for short pilgrimages within one's own realm, as in the case of an English person making the popular journey from London to Canterbury. A serf who had to get his lord's permission to leave his duties for several days probably constituted one exception to this rule. Pilgrims going on longer journeys to foreign lands, however, found it advisable to obtain a certificate from their local bishop. In a sense, pilgrims visiting a distant shrine were conducting spiritual business and church leaders maintained and exercised their authority to watch over and guide any such business involving members of their flocks.

A certificate from a bishop also had practical value for a traveler. Such a document not only gave the pilgrim permission to visit, for instance, Rome or Jerusalem, but also offered a certain amount of protection if the pilgrim got into trouble along the way. If some local foreign official or clergyman questioned a traveler's identity or wrongly suspected him or her of some offense, the certificate, constituting a set of proper credentials, might keep the pilgrim from being thrown in jail. One such certificate that has survived reads: "William de Hornby granted letter of protection for pilgrimage to St. James' shrine; 20s. [20 shillings] for expenses.—July 17, 1368."[33]

The prospective traveler next either made or bought a standard pilgrim's outfit, recognized as such all over the Mediterranean world in medieval times. "This," explains Louise Collis, "consisted of a long grey robe with a hood, a broad-brimmed hat marked with a red cross, the scrip, or little satchel for provisions, a water bottle and a long staff to lean on at rough places, or at the end of the day."[34] Pilgrims also regularly wore little tokens or badges that they received at the various shrines they visited. Each of these souvenirs was unique. The token from Saint Thomas Becket's shrine at Canterbury was a tiny ampulla, or flask, of holy water; the badge from the shrine honoring Saint James in Spain was shaped like a scallop shell; and the badge a pilgrim was entitled to wear after completing a voyage to Jerusalem and the Holy Land was shaped like a palm leaf, giving rise to the term "palmer" to describe such a pilgrim.

Phony Pilgrims

Those who went on numerous pilgrimages during their lifetimes proudly displayed their tokens and badges, covering their pilgrim's robes, because they brought a person much attention and prestige. In some cases they were also worth a certain amount of money. Poor beggars often pleaded with pilgrims to give them these objects, or even stole them, so

A medieval pilgrim prays at the door of a local church, perhaps in preparation for his departure for a distant shrine.

that they could wear them and thereby pretend they had made the pilgrimages themselves. It was common for very devout people of means to give substantial handouts to what they assumed were reverent, honorable pilgrims who had fallen on bad times. The following description of one of these phony pilgrims comes from the *Vision of Piers the Plowman* by the fourteenth-century English poet William Langland:

> He bore him a [pilgrim's] staff, with a broad strip bound. . . . A bowl and a bag [scrip] he bore by his side; a hundred of vials [tokens and badges] was set on his hat, signs from Sinai [in the Holy Land], Spanish [scallop] shells; with crosses on his cloak, and keys [badge symbols] of Rome. . . . Then gladly would [a passerby] ask from whence he [the beggar] had

come? "From Sinai," he said, "and the Holy Sepulcher, Bethlehem and Babylon, I've been in them both, Armenia, Alexandria, and other like [similar] places. You may see by the signs that here sit on my hat [that] I have walked full widely, in wet and in dry [weather], and sought our good saints for the health of my soul."[35]

The Send-Off

Once all the preparations for a pilgrimage had been made, it was time for the send-off. Sometimes this was a small and rather private affair, as in the case of Margery Kempe. Shortly before boarding ship in the English port of Yarmouth in the winter of 1413–1414, she visited the cathedral in the nearby town of Norwich, where a local priest said a prayer for her. She herself prayed at the altar, then joined her husband in Yarmouth, told him good-bye, and embarked.

For other pilgrims, taking leave involved a great deal more ceremony. A crowd of relatives and friends might line the docks, offering prayers, extra money for the trip, and food to eat on the boat. When a departing traveler belonged to a guild, either a craft or mercantile association similar in some ways to a modern labor union, or a charitable organization connected to a church, each of the other members was expected to make a contribution and to join in the send-off. A surviving public record of guild activities in the English town of Lincoln dating from 1350 reads:

The Corpus Christi Gild [Guild] of St. Michael on the Hill, Lincoln, founded in 1350, ordained that if a member went on pilgrimage to Jerusalem, each brother should give him 1d [1 penny]. If he went to St. James [in Spain] or to St. Peter and St. Paul [in Rome], all the brethren [of the guild] should lead him to the Cross

A Medieval Itinerary

Here, quoted in Chaucer's World, *is an itinerary, or record of a journey, compiled by a writer named Adam of Usk after he made a pilgrimage from London to Rome in the winter of 1401–1402.*

"On the nineteenth day of February [1402], I . . . took ship at Billingsgate in London and with a favoring wind crossed the sea [English Channel], and, within the space of a day landing at Bergen-op-Zoom in Brabant [now in the Netherlands], the country which I sought, I set my face towards Rome. Thence passing through Diest, Maastricht, Aachen, Cologn, Bonn,

Coblentz, Worms, Speyer, Strassburg . . . Basil, Bern, Lucerne, and its wonderful lake, Mont St. Gotthard, and the hermitage [religious retreat] on its summit . . . I arrived at Bellinzona in Lombardy [northern Italy]. Thence through Como, Milan, Piacenza . . . Pisa, Siena . . . turning aside from Bologna, Florence, and Perugia on account of the raging wars and sieges of the Duke of Milan . . . and halting two days at every best inn for refreshment of myself and men and still more of my horses, on the fifth day of April by the favor of God . . . I came safely through all to Rome."

before the Hospital of the Holy Innocents without [outside of] Lincoln, and when he returned should meet him there and bring him to the Mother Church [main cathedral] of Lincoln.[36]

In some cases the person who initiated and organized a pilgrimage, the nominal pilgrim, did the sending off. It was a common custom to engage in "pilgrimage by proxy"—that is, to hire or ask someone else to make the actual trip in one's place—to fulfill a promise made to a deceased relative or friend. The belief was that if someone, even a stranger, made a journey to a holy shrine and prayed for the dead person, that person's soul benefited; so some surviving relatives, having neither the time nor the desire to make such a trip themselves, got someone else to go. Many people placed requests for such pilgrimages in their wills and even left behind money to cover the proxy's expenses. For example, an English knight left this request in his will:

> May 2, 1388. John de Multon, knight.— My body to be buried in the Monastery of the Blessed Mary of Lincoln. . . . Item, I bequeath [leave] to one man going for my soul as far as Jerusalem, 5 marks.[37]

And a clause in a London merchant's will read:

> February 10, 1394. John Blakeney, citizen and fishmonger of London, buried at Charterhouse.—I bequeath 20 marks to hire one chaplain to go on pilgrimage to Rome and there to remain throughout one year, to celebrate and pray for my soul and the souls for whom I am bound [to pray], and £10 [10 pounds] to hire two men to go on pilgrimage for my soul to St. James in Galicia [a section of northern Spain], to fulfill my vow.[38]

These and many other similar medieval wills testify to the extreme importance most people placed on holy shrines, prayer, and salvation and constitute still further evidence of the strength and depth of Christian faith all over Europe.

An Endless Flow of Travelers

After the send-off, the pilgrim left behind the comforts, safety, and familiarity of home and began a new adventure on the much less comfortable, less safe, and less familiar roads crisscrossing the European realms. He or she was rarely alone, of course. Groups of pilgrims, such as the one Chaucer described, were the rule and it was common to encounter other groups, as well as merchants, messengers, and a colorful collection of other travelers, along the way. According to Pulitzer Prize–winning historian Barbara W. Tuchman:

> The rutted roads, always either too dusty or too muddy, carried an endless flow of pilgrims and peddlers, merchants, with their packtrains, bishops making visitations, tax-collectors and royal officials, friars and pardoners, wandering scholars, jongleurs [minstrels and entertainers] and preachers, messengers and couriers who wove the network of communications from city to city. Great nobles . . . bankers, prelates [high-ranking clergymen], abbeys [monasteries], courts of justice, town governments, kings and their councils employed their own messengers.[39]

Pilgrims usually had a general idea of how long it would take to get from one town,

Many pilgrims traveled in groups, both for companionship and for mutual protection, as in this drawing depicting Chaucer's famous band of travelers.

inn, or shrine to another. If this was their first pilgrimage or trip away from home, they had already interviewed veteran pilgrims to learn the ropes, so they knew, for instance, that it took about twenty days to walk the length of France, from Flanders in the far north to Navarre in the far south. Using other established rule-of-thumb walking times, pilgrims and other travelers also knew it would take about sixteen days to traverse France from west to east; five to seven days to make it through the Mont Cenis pass in the Alps, the most common route into Italy from northern and western Europe; and about five weeks to go from Paris to Naples, then a quaint seaside town south of Rome.

One major concern during such long journeys was finding suitable and safe lodg-

ings each night. Thankfully for the pilgrims, this was only rarely a problem, for a whole network of such hospices existed across Europe for the benefit of travelers, especially holy pilgrims. Because many pilgrims preferred places where they could worship as well as eat and sleep, churches, monasteries, and convents became popular lodgings, sanctuaries that were safe and quiet, and where local priests and nuns were sympathetic with their beliefs and goals.

A great demand grew for these church hospices. After the turning of the first millennium—that is, the year 1000—Europe experienced an upsurge in trade, commerce, population, and town building. All of these factors helped to expand prosperity and also to stimulate increased travel, including pilgrimages. Partly in response to the growing demand for spiritual rest stops, Europe underwent a massive burst of church building in the eleventh century, during which 1,587 new churches sprang up in France alone. Raoul Glaber, a monk of the time, remarked, "It was as though the very world had shaken herself and cast off her old age, and were clothing herself everywhere in a white garment of churches."[40]

Other Places to Stay

Pilgrims could also stop for rest and food at castles on well-to-do manors. According to the Scriptures, good Christians were supposed to take in travelers in need and manorial lords generally offered their hospitality, even when they suspected their guests might only be beggars pretending to be pilgrims. In *Life on a Medieval Barony*, William S. Davis writes:

Every day they appear at the gate of St. Aliquis castle [in France] to ask a share in the supper and a bed . . . in the hall, and they are respectfully treated, although Conon [the castle's lord] sometimes complains that their trailing robes of brown wool, heavy staffs, and sacks [scrips] slung at belt are merely the disguises for so many wandering rogues. Unwashed and unkempt though many of them are, it never does to repulse them [turn them away], lest you lose the Scriptural blessing for those who received strangers and so "have entertained angels unawares."[41]

Of course, some pilgrims opted to pay for lodgings at inns, such as Chaucer's Tabard Inn, many of which existed on the roadways. Others, because they were low on funds or did not want to associate with the merchants, soldiers, and other roving characters who frequented these spots, preferred a free bed in a quiet church or monastery. Another option

A group of pilgrims departs a country village after having spent the night at a local inn.

for those who wanted only the company of other pilgrims was a pilgrim hostel, designed specifically for religious travelers. Various organizations, including guilds, operated such inexpensive, spare, but congenial lodgings, one of which is described in this English public record dating from 1340: "The Gild Merchant of Coventry provided a hostel with thirteen beds for poor men passing on pilgrimage. A governor [manager] presided over it, and there was a woman to keep it clean. The upkeep was £10 a year."[42]

"Let's Not Grow Moldy Thus in Idleness"

Pilgrims had plenty to keep them busy, both at night in their lodgings and in the daytime on the road. Evenings were often spent writing long letters to family and friends back home, inquiring how things were there and also describing the sites and experiences of the trip. There was no formal postage service, so most letters had to be carried by merchants; visiting bishops, priests, and monks; pilgrims homeward bound; or other travelers, which meant that such correspondence moved unreliably and very slowly. For example, it typically took a month for a letter to go across a country the size of France or Italy. However, few complained, for, as scholar Charles de la Ronciere points out:

> Everyone was aware of the difficulties. The delays only made letters more precious to those who received them, and correspondence was composed with the slowness of transit in mind. The correspondent was kept abreast of intimate household affairs. . . . Letters were sometimes warmer than conversation would have been. In writing one was forced to

find words to express affection, anxiety . . . relief, and joy, words that came less easily to women's lips . . . owing to convention [custom] and modesty.[43]

Another activity that frequently occupied a pilgrim's time was poring over the many available guidebooks and conversational manuals. Long pilgrimages took travelers to distant countries where the languages were often strange, so language manuals were necessary and invaluable tools that enabled them to ask directions, order food, and so forth. Following is an excerpt from a conversational manual, dated from about 1400, written for Germans traveling in France:

To ask the right road:

> "Sir, God give you good day," or "God give you good health and good luck," or "Madame, God give you good evening," or "God commend you and guard you from evil, my friend." = "Sir, you are welcome."
> "What hour of the day is it?". . . = "Between six and seven."
> "How far is it from here to Paris?" = "Twelve leagues and far enough.". . .
> "Of these two, is this the right road?" = "God help me, sweet sir, no."
> To make enquiry [inquiry] concerning lodgings:
> "Madame, have you lodging for us three fellows?" = "Sir, how long would you stay?"
> "Madame, we don't know." = "Then what would you pay for your board by the day?"
> "Madame, what would you take for each of us?" = "Sir, not less than six pence [pennies] a day."
> "Madame, we are willing to pay that." = "Sir, by God you are welcome."[44]

Of course, while walking along the road for hours or sitting at dinner in an inn, hostel, or church hall, the most common pastime was conversation with one's fellow travelers. The stories told by Chaucer's pilgrims are the most obvious example. Seeing that the trek is getting a bit boring, the host, Harry Bailly, exclaims:

A quarter of this present day is gone;
Now for the love of God and of Saint
    John,
Lose no more time, or [as] little as you
    may;
Masters, the time is wasting night and
    day. . . .
Let's not grow moldy thus in idleness.
"Sir Lawyer," said he, "as you have hope
    of bliss,
Tell us a tale, as our agreement is."[45]

Medieval pilgrims spent many pleasant hours chatting and telling stories. But sometimes, if one of the group became obnoxious, the conversation and even the whole mood of the trip could turn sour. "One of many practical tips given by contemporary guide books," writes Collis, "is the absolute necessity of keeping on good terms with one's company. Pilgrim quarrels were notoriously bitter. Give offense to no one, the prospective traveler is advised, for you will only get the worst of it." Margery Kempe learned this lesson the hard way. Her faith was such an all-consuming obsession that she talked constantly and exclusively about God, heaven, salvation, and repentance, making her traveling companions at first bored, then irritated, and finally angry. To them, Collis states, "she seemed to go too far. They felt that there were many interesting subjects to discuss besides heaven. Particularly at dinner, they objected to her monologue. They were sick of her visions and boastings of holiness."[46] Eventually, they insisted that she sit at the end of the table away from them and keep her mouth shut.

Margery was lucky in a way. The falling-out with her companions was the only notable mishap on her trip from England to the Holy Land. For the most part, this pilgrimage, her first, was successful because it was uneventful. So much could and did go wrong on these journeys that many other pilgrims were not so fortunate.

Medieval Mishaps and Mayhem: When Pilgrimages Went Wrong

No matter how well-meaning the pilgrims or how carefully they planned their trips, pilgrimages sometimes suffered mishaps or even ended in disaster. Of course, many dangers risked in foreign towns and lands were no different from those people faced at home. For example, some pilgrims suffered fatal accidents while simply walking the streets of a foreign city. A surviving record from the office of a London coroner, dated 1337, describes the sort of hit-and-run accident that was not uncommon in larger cities:

> On Thursday [February 13], about the hour of vespers, two carters [cart drivers] taking two empty carts outside of the city were urging their horses apace [to speed], when the wheels of one of the carts collapsed opposite the . . . hospital of St. Mary, Bishopsgate, so that the cart fell on Agnes de Cicestre, who immediately died. The carter thereupon left his cart and three horses and took flight in fear, although he was not suspected of malicious [evil] intent.[47]

Other common accidents pilgrims suffered included losing their footing and plunging off hillsides; plummeting into ravines, rivers, or lakes; and falling overboard when on sea voyages.

Although a relatively small proportion of pilgrims met with such accidents, many oth-ers fell prey to a host of other more common dangers. These included disease, the causes of and cures for which were little understood in that era; poor sanitation, about which most people were equally ignorant; fires, famines, avalanches, and other natural disasters; and attacks by wild animals and highwaymen. Plagued by one or more of these problems, many pilgrimages were unsuccessful or end-ed in tragedy. Other pilgrims eventually made it to their intended destinations only after suffering much hardship and misery.

An Intolerable Stench

Poor sanitation and contaminated water cer-tainly took its toll of travelers, especially first-time pilgrims who did not know what to expect or to watch out for when in unfamiliar locales. Poisoning caused by drinking conta-minated water was especially prevalent. The standard tests people used to determine if water was safe to drink were looking and smelling; that is, as long as the water looked clear and did not smell bad they assumed it was all right to consume. The concept of germs was unknown in medieval times, of course, so no one suspected that invisible microorganisms existed in streams, lakes, and wells. Most of these germs were harmless or caused no more than minor stomach upset, but others, even when the water looked clear

In this engraving of a medieval street scene, a woman empties her chamber pot into the street, a decidedly unsanitary but quite common practice of that era.

and smelled fine, could be deadly. This was particularly true when people routinely dumped raw sewage into the nearest lake or stream, a fairly common practice. Residents of a given area quickly learned which water sources were safe and which were not, but unless these locals erected signs or other warning markers a visiting band of thirsty pilgrims had no way of telling the safe sources from the polluted ones.

In general, poor sanitation was a problem everywhere in Europe in an age when people dumped their garbage and sewage not only into streams, but into street gutters and backyards as well. Such practices promoted the growth of disease germs, which contributed to rates of sickness and death considerably higher than today's. But in this regard pilgrims were at no greater risk than anyone else.

For travelers, including pilgrims, lack of sanitation became a much more serious problem on ships, on which many people were closely confined for long periods of time. Louise Collis describes the conditions in which pilgrims lived on such voyages:

The general cabin for pilgrims was the hold under the rowing deck. There were no portholes. Light and air came only through the hatchways. A berth consisted of a space big enough to lie down in chalked [outlined in chalk] on the boards. This would be one's only private place during the voyage. Here one spread one's mattress, piled one's luggage at its foot and tried to sleep through the noise of snoring, cursing, talking, the sailors running about overhead, the animals in pens on deck stamping, all the creaking and movement of a ship at sea. The heat and smell were horrible.[48]

Much worse than the cramped space, noise, heat, and foul smells was the problem of eliminating bodily wastes. Felix Faber, a Dominican monk who traveled to the Holy Land twice, in 1480 and 1483, left behind a graphic record of what he and his fellow pilgrims endured on the boat ride. "A ripe turd is an unbearable burden," he began.

Each pilgrim has by his bed a urinal—a vessel of terracotta, a small bottle—into which he urinates and vomits. But since the quarters are cramped for the number of people, and dark besides . . . it is seldom that these vessels are not overturned before dawn. Quite regularly, in

fact . . . some clumsy fellow will knock over five or six urinals in passing, giving rise to an intolerable stench.

Faber went on to describe how in the morning the travelers would go up on deck and line up to use the few "privies," portable toilets that channeled the wastes directly overboard, provided by the crew.

Sometimes as many as thirteen people or more will line up for a turn at the seat. But the difficulties become really serious in bad weather, when the privies are constantly inundated by waves. . . . To go to the seat in the middle of a storm is thus to risk being completely soaked, so that many passengers remove their clothing and go stark naked.

While on pilgrimage to Jerusalem in 1035, the Duke of Normandy suddenly becomes ill. Sickness and disease were common hazards of these long and arduous journeys.

To help relieve the problem of human wastes and vomit building up in the hold where people slept, Faber advised pilgrims to

> go to the privies three or four times every day, even when there is no natural urge . . . and do not lose hope if nothing comes [out] on the third or fourth try. Go often, loosen your belt, untie all the knots of your clothes over chest and stomach, and evacuation will occur even if your intestines are filled with stones. This advice was given me by an old sailor once when I had been terribly constipated for several days.[49]

Needless to say, exposed to such unsanitary conditions, large numbers of pilgrims bound for Jerusalem must have contracted hepatitis, a serious inflammation of the liver.

Thieves, Rapists, and Swindlers

Another hazard pilgrims routinely faced took the form of highwaymen, pirates, and a whole range of swindlers and other unethical individuals who preyed on travelers. Highwaymen regularly robbed pilgrims of money, jewelry, food, horses, and other goods and sometimes, if they put up a fight, murdered them. A surviving English court record, dated 1398, states that on January 20 of that year, "John Suoring, alias [also called] John Gelle of Walsingham, at night killed Geoffrey Blogate of Norfolk and took goods . . . to the value of £10 from his purse and is a common thief."[50] Highwaymen were also known to rape women who took the chance of traveling alone, as this court record shows: "Thomas Walsham, alias Coke, late canon [clergyman]

Negotiating for Common Comforts

The hazards and discomforts pilgrims experienced aboard ships bound for Jerusalem and other shrines around Europe could be lessened somewhat by making sure to insert special clauses in the contracts they signed with the ship captains. According to Louise Collis in Memoirs of a Medieval Woman, *clauses could be included*

to restrain the captain from trying to combine pilgrims with merchandise, which was, in any case, forbidden by law. Chests of goods were not to be intruded into the pilgrims' cabin, taking up space already paid for dearly enough. . . . On account of seasickness, overcrowding, rats, lice, fleas, maggots, [and] foul air . . . travelers often fell ill. One should try to provide for such times: the captain must definitely con-

cede the right [for pilgrims] to come up on deck for air at any hour and to remain there until revived. If the worst happened and one died, one's belongings were not to be seized from those to whom one had willed them. Also, a proportion of the passage money ought to be returned. It might not be possible to get him to agree to carry one's body to the nearest land for proper burial, because a corpse on a ship was considered unlucky by sailors. They preferred to pitch it overboard. Lastly, the captain should be asked to give protection against violence from the crew, especially the oarsman. These were not usually slaves . . . but a sort of conscript, notoriously rough, brutal and inclined to settle any argument in the most primitive manner.

A band of medieval highwaymen attack an unfortunate group of travelers. Pilgrims regularly faced the threat of robbery, rape, and even murder.

of Walsingham . . . raped against her will, Emma, wife of William Bole of Walsingham, coming on pilgrimage to Canterbury, and took goods . . . from her purse to the value of £20, and is a common thief."[51]

Pirates, of course, constituted the equivalent of highwaymen on the seas. Pilgrims traveling from the British Isles to continental Europe or from southern Europe to the Holy Land always ran the risk of running into fast and deadly pirate galleys that seemed to appear from nowhere. Abbot Guibert described a group of pilgrims who had a run-in with a pirate vessel in the English Channel in 1113:

> When they [the pilgrims] had traveled to the Channel, they found certain wealthy merchants with ships for that voyage and were carried across calmly, as far as the winds were concerned. But suddenly they saw the galleys of pirates, whom they greatly feared, coming on directly against them. Steering toward them with oars sweeping the waters and their prows cutting through the waves, they were soon scarcely a furlong [about 220 yards] off. As the carriers of the [holy] relics were terribly afraid of those marine soldiers, one of our priests arose from their midst and lifted on high the reliquary [container for relics] . . . forbidding their approach in the name of the Son [Christ] and of the Mother [Mary]. At that command the pirate craft immediately fell astern [back], driven off as speedily as they had with eagerness approached.[52]

These pilgrims were fortunate to have encountered pirates who feared for their souls if they violated holy relics. Many travelers were not so fortunate and suffered robbery and/or death at the hands of less superstitious villains.

Less lethal but just as dishonest were swindlers who preyed on pilgrims at inns and taverns, on crowded city streets, or at the sacred shrines themselves. Counterfeiters, crooks who manufactured fake money, took advantage of the confusion when large numbers of pilgrims congregated and passed around their phony currency. According to the Winstons:

> Tricksters also had some famous routines for swindling travelers at inns. First one man would appear lamenting that he had just lost a valuable chain or ring. After he had left, his accomplice would turn up and offer to sell a chain or ring he had just found at a price far below the value mentioned by the first man. . . . Cardsharps and players with loaded dice abounded in the taverns, while cutpurses [thieves who grabbed purses and ran] and pickpockets prowled the streets.[53]

In addition, false pilgrims, their hats and robes covered with stolen tokens and badges, abounded at the more popular shrines. These beggars were experts at telling tragic stories in order to win the sympathies of real pilgrims. They became such a nuisance in Rome in the late 1300s that King Charles VI of France passed a law forbidding French pilgrims from traveling to Rome without a sealed and authentic license issued by the government. Anyone who could not produce this license when ordered to do so was immediately thrown into prison.

"I Would That I Had Never Been Born"

Natural disasters of various kinds also took a toll on pilgrims. For instance, in an age when no weather forecasting existed, ship travelers rarely had any advance warning that a dangerous storm was heading their way. Some boats capsized in sudden heavy seas and most

or all of the crew and passengers drowned. Because of the power exerted by faith in that age, those who survived such storms usually attributed their deliverance to God's or some saint's favor, as reported in this surviving English guild record from 1365:

> Five men had vowed a pilgrimage to the land of St. James [northern Spain], and while returning after its completion were in great danger from a storm at sea. They vowed that, if by the intercession [intervention] of St. James they were preserved . . . they would build in his honor an altar. . . . When they had made their vow, the storm ceased.[54]

True to their vow, the men built the altar.

Other natural hazards and disasters that befell pilgrims included local famines, which made it difficult for travelers to find sufficient food in some areas; avalanches, most frequently in the Alpine passes on the way to or from Rome or Venice; as well as mudslides, rockslides, earthquakes, and forest fires.

Far worse than these scattered and relatively infrequent occurrences, however, was the threat of infectious disease. Two of the most feared illnesses that one could contract while traveling in a strange land were erysipelas, called Saint Anthony's fire, an acute skin condition; and leprosy, which caused the body to erupt in disfiguring sores and ulcers.

But even these dreaded diseases paled in significance before the frightening onslaught of the bubonic plague, known as the Black Death. Caused by a germ that infected fleas, which infested rats, which then spread the disease through human communities, the plague was called "black" in reference to the dark blotches that covered the body as blood pooled and dried under the skin. Typically, the symptoms of the disease were terrible pain, spitting up blood, and egg-sized swellings called buboes in the groin and under the armpits, usually followed by death, all occurring within a week or less.

The plague struck first in the Crimea, along the northern edge of the Black Sea, in 1346, where it killed an estimated 85,000 people in less than three months. Traders from the Italian city of Genoa then carried the pestilence to their homeland and in the next few years it spread with alarming speed all across Europe. The death toll was horrendous. Some 63,000 people died in Naples, Italy, in the space of two months, while more than 100,000 succumbed in the northern Italian city of Florence, and numerous other towns lost as many as three quarters of their

Relatives congregate at the bedside of a plague victim. Because they were ignorant of its causes, medieval people's attempts to cure or stop the spread of the disease were generally useless.

Giovanni Boccaccio, the noted Italian writer who vividly depicted the onslaught of the Black Death in his Decameron *tales.*

inhabitants. "On all sides is sorrow," lamented the Italian writer Petrarch in a 1348 letter to his brother. "Everywhere is fear. I would that I had never been born, or, at least had died before these times."[55] Petrarch's contemporary, the famous Italian writer Giovanni Boccaccio, captured the staggering scale and horror of the disaster in this passage from his *Decameron*:

> Many dropped dead in the open streets, both by day and by night, while a great many others, though dying in their own houses, drew their neighbors' attention to the fact more by the smell of their rotting

corpses than by any other means. And what with these, and the others, who were dying all over the city, bodies were here, there, and everywhere. So when all the graves were full, huge trenches were excavated in the churchyards, into which new arrivals were placed in their hundreds, stowed tier upon tier like ships' cargo, each layer of corpses being covered over with a thin layer of soil till the trench was filled to the top. . . . No more respect was accorded to dead people that would nowadays be shown toward dead goats.[56]

In all, according to modern estimates, as many as 25 million people, about one-third the population of Europe, perished in this initial plague outbreak alone. At least five smaller but still deadly secondary outbreaks ravaged Europe between 1355 and 1400 and several more struck without warning in the following two centuries.

Desperate Measures

The plague affected holy pilgrims in various ways. First, when passing through unfamiliar towns on their way to distant shrines, they took the risk of encountering new pockets of plague victims and thereby of catching the disease. Conversely, some towns shut them out, along with all other strangers. For example, in 1348, in a desperate effort to fend off the dreaded disease, Pistoia, Lucca, and several other Italian towns adopted strict quarantines, and in the next thirty years many other European communities did the same. Some of these measures were moderately successful; others had little effect. In any case, pilgrims denied entry into safer areas were often unable to find uncontaminated food or lodgings within areas covering many

square miles. Some managed eventually to reach their destinations but then contracted the plague while at the shrines or on the return trip and never made it home. Those who did make it home frequently found most of their relatives and friends dead or dying from the pestilence.

God's Wrath

It was perhaps an ironic twist that the plague not only killed, widowed, orphaned, or badly inconvenienced pilgrims, but also greatly stimulated people's desire to go on pilgrimages in the first place. This seeming contradiction stemmed from popular beliefs about the cause of the disease. Since no one knew about germs, the explanations offered by learned authorities were shrouded in ignorance and fantasy. One scholar, Pope Clement VI's physician, Guy de Chauliac, declared that a conjunction, or clustering together in the sky, of the planets Mars, Saturn, and Jupiter, which had been observed in 1345, had spawned the plague by "corrupting" the earth's atmosphere. Faculty members at the University of Paris suggested that unseen celestial disturbances had overheated the ocean near India, releasing "noxious vapors" that somehow caused the plague.

But most people ultimately rejected such theories. In an age obsessed with the concepts of God, sin, and salvation, the vast majority embraced what they saw as the only plausible explanation for a disaster of such magnitude—God's wrath. Boccaccio recorded the widespread belief that the plague "was a punishment signifying God's righteous anger at our iniquitous [sinful] way of life."[57] In the medieval mind, holy pilgrimage was one widely accepted way to appease God or to gain his forgiveness and mercy; therefore,

the more the plague ravaged humanity, the more people felt compelled to march along the roads of Europe seeking salvation.

Some of these holy travelers, driven by fear and blind devotion into a religious frenzy, marched randomly from town to town with no specific destination. The most famous of these bizarre pilgrims were the Flagellants, who appeared first in Germany in 1349 and then quickly spread across Europe. Trying to persuade God to forgive humanity, to convince people in the towns they visited to repent, and by these means end the plague, three times each day they stripped down to their underwear and beat themselves and each other with whips until they collapsed bleeding. And all the while they chanted: "Our journey's done in the holy name. Christ Himself to Jerusalem came. His cross He bore in His holy hand. Help us, Savior of all the land. . . . Come [we] here for penance good and well, thus we escape from burning hell."[58]

The way people reacted to the plague illustrates why neither this disaster, nor

(Above) In this symbolic depiction, the "demon of the bubonic plague" infects another pathetic victim. (Right) A group of Flagellants, gluttons for self-punishment, parade through a town calling on the inhabitants to repent.

Ghostly Outlines of a Vanished People

In this excerpt from his essay "The Black Death: 1347–50," in The End of the World: A History, *scholar Otto Friedrich describes how whole towns were depopulated during the major outbreak of bubonic plague that struck Europe in the 1340s.*

A medieval doctor makes a vain attempt to rid his patient of the dreaded plague.

"One would think that any disaster that killed 25 million people in Europe alone would leave the entire Continent paralyzed for at least a generation. If the streets of New York City were suddenly littered with a corresponding number of corpses, roughly two million, or if the United States as a whole suffered more than fifty million deaths by bubonic plague within three years, the process of recovery would be hard to imagine. And so it is that we retain from the chronicles of the fourteenth century an image of deserted cottages falling in ruins and untilled wheat fields reverting to wilderness. Thousands of villages all across the face of Europe did simply disappear. The buried remnants are faintly visible in aerial photographs, spectral [ghostly] outlines of a vanished people, and in England alone more than two thousand such ruins have been recorded. The Germans even have a word, *Dorfwüstungen*, for the process of villages turning into wilderness. The depopulation of the cities was no less remarkable. In Toulouse [in southern France], to take only one example, the number of inhabitants not only shrank from an estimated 30,000 in 1335 to 26,000 in 1385 but continued shrinking to 20,700 in 1398 and 8,000 in 1430. Virtually no city anywhere regained its population of [the year] 1300 in less than two centuries."

storms, nor avalanches, nor ship holds mired in human waste, nor pirates and highwaymen, nor any other dire threat was enough to deter the spirit of holy pilgrimage. God was the most potent and motivating force in most people's lives. Suffering any pain or ordeal was not only worth it but necessary, for one's existence on earth was seen as only part of a journey toward salvation in heaven, which was all that mattered in the long run. The fourteenth-century poet Guillaume de Guilleville summed up the medieval meaning of life in a single phrase: "Your life here [on earth] is but a pilgrimage [to God's kingdom]." [59]

Reaching a Spiritual Goal: Europe's Many Sacred Shrines and Relics

The end goals of pilgrimages such as the one described by Chaucer were the holy shrines, where pilgrims prayed, sought salvation, or just tried in their own individual ways to feel closer to God. What exactly did medieval pilgrims see and do at these shrines? In *The Canterbury Tales*, Chaucer described how the pilgrims amused themselves on their way to Canterbury Cathedral but offered no specifics about the shrine itself or what the travelers did when they arrived there. An anonymous fifteenth-century document, *The Tale of Beryn*, intended as a continuation of Chaucer's incomplete *Tales*, provided some of these specifics, stating that the pilgrims

> Kneeled down before the shrine, said
>   heartily their prayer;
> They prayed to St. Thomas [Becket] in
>   such wise [ways] as they knew,
> And then the holy relics, each man
>   kissed them, too,
> As from the goodly monk [attending the
>   shrine] the name of each they learned;
> And then to other places of holiness they
>   turned,
> And were at their devotions till the
>   service was sung through.[60]

The shrine of Saint Thomas Becket was one of the most famous in Europe and attracted pilgrims from many lands. Yet a person could have gone on a different and equally gratifying pilgrimage every year of his or her life without once making it to Becket's shrine. Literally hundreds of shrines, most less renowned but no less sacred than Canterbury, and each with its supposedly one-of-a-kind relics, were scattered across the Mediterranean world. So many people visited these sites between the eleventh and fifteenth centuries that at any given time as many as fifty to one hundred thousand pilgrims might be trekking the roads of Europe in various directions. And the volume of traffic was much higher during certain holy times of the year such as recognized Christian holidays and local religious festivals.

Relics Lure the Faithful

Shrines attracted pilgrims for various reasons, one of the most important being the sacred relics they housed. Some of the most common types of relics were bones, teeth, mummified feet and hands, and other body parts said to have belonged to famous biblical figures and Christian saints; clothes and personal effects once owned or handled by these holy people; and pieces of the "true cross," the cross, according to the Scriptures, on which Christ was crucified. Some artifacts belonging to secular figures were also revered as relics, among them the hunting

These relics in the Basilica of Saint Mark in Venice consist of metal containers said to hold the arms of fourteenth- and fifteenth-century saints.

horn of the eighth-century French hero Roland and the sword of his contemporary, the French king Charlemagne.

Because the authenticity of these objects was rarely, if ever, documented, pilgrims had no way of knowing if they were real or phony. But in that age of deep and unswerving faith, it was almost unheard-of to question the claims made by the keepers of the holy shrines. Most people simply accepted these claims at face value and viewed the relics with a mixture of religious reverence and superstitious awe. As writer Michael Kuh points out:

Relics buttressed [strengthened] faith. Men took oaths on them, [and] through them sought to cure illness, avert the evil eye, stop a plague, ensure a good harvest. Greatly valued (merchants of Venice paid the king of Jerusalem 20,000 gold coins for a newly found piece of the True Cross), they were often housed in costly reliquaries [containers]. Louis IX [of France] built an entire church, Paris's beautiful Sainte Chapelle, to house a thorn from the crown [of thorns] Christ wore [while being crucified].[61]

Pieces of the true cross, crown of thorns, and other items associated directly with Christ were, not surprisingly, the most sought after and awe-inspiring of all medieval relics. Numerous churches claimed to possess such sacred objects. For example, the Church of

A fifteenth-century miniature depicts a procession of church officials bearing holy relics.

Christ being crucified (left), and suffering the pain of the crown of thorns. Many medieval churches claimed to house pieces of the cross or one or more of the thorns.

Saint Croix in Provins, France, boasted that it had a fragment of the cross, as did a church in Troyes, France; Saint Paul's Cathedral in London; and many others. An English knight, Richard Poynings, claimed to own a large piece of the true cross and willed it to his family and local church:

> I bequeath to my beloved wife, Lady of Arundel and Maltravers, a cross containing a large piece of the Holy Cross. This is now in pledge [on loan]; when it is recovered, each of my children is to have a piece, with the divine blessing . . . but my wife is to have the larger piece for her life. Afterwards [that is, after his wife and children died] the cross and the larger piece of the Holy Cross [are] to go to the church of Stokecours, forever.[62]

Other relics associated with Christ included bits of his robe on display in Vézelay in central France; the basin in which he washed his disciples' feet, in Troyes; one of the jars in which he turned water to wine, in Venice; a stone from his tomb, a stone from Mount Calvary where the cross stood, and still another stone said to be from the spot where he ascended into heaven, all in London; and parts of the crown of thorns, in Paris. A number of churches across Europe even claimed to own Christ's baby teeth and the foreskin of his penis discarded during his circumcision but offered no explanation of how and why such items could have been preserved.

Outside of the items attributed to Christ, the most popular relics were those associated with the Virgin Mary and various saints and biblical figures. The church at Vézelay supposedly had a number of such objects, including hairs from Mary's head, a bone once belonging to John the Baptist, the man who had baptized Christ, and the church's most prized possession—the mummified body of Mary Magdalene, the fallen woman who had become Christ's devoted follower. Troyes featured a skull said to be that of Saint Philip and Canterbury claimed to house

Relics Abound

In this excerpt from his book Life on a Medieval Barony, *historian William S. Davis discusses the ways in which various Western churches and individuals acquired their relics.*

"Saints' relics abound. Where is the monastery, church, or even castle without them? Sometimes they rest in golden caskets in the very place where the holy personages departed this life. Sometimes they have been brought from Rome or Palestine by pious pilgrims; very often they come as gifts. The direct purchase of relics is somewhat sacrilegious [unholy], but you can present a king, duke, or great ecclesiastic [church official] with a good relic just as you give him some hawks or ermine skins—as a reward for favors past and expected. The Pope is always sending desirable relics to bishops and abbots whom he wishes to honor; and, as all know, after the Latins [Europeans] sacked Constantinople in 1204 [during the Fourth Crusade] there was hardly a shrine in all France which did not get the skull, a few ribs, or even the entire body of some Eastern saint. The booty in relics, in fact, was almost as important as that of gold and jewels."

pieces of Saint Thomas's brains (dashed out by Henry's knights), as well as one of Saint Margaret's feet. And various churches in Venice had one of Saint George's arms, Saint Nicholas's staff, one of Saint Paul's ears, and a tooth belonging to Goliath, the giant warrior slain by the shepherd boy David, later king of Israel.

Most of the many relics in Western churches and shrines came from the lands of the eastern Mediterranean. Some were donated or even bought, but a large number were stolen or captured during the Crusades. According to William S. Davis, when the European nobles sacked Constantinople, in what is now Turkey, in 1204 during the Fourth Crusade, "there was hardly a shrine in all France which did not get the skull, a few ribs, or even the entire body of some Eastern saint. The booty in relics, in fact, was almost as important as that of gold and jewels."[63]

Such relics regularly drew crowds of the faithful to various churches and shrines, where these pilgrims were often overcome with awe and emotion. Margery Kempe's August 1414 visit to the Church of Saint Francis in Assisi, Italy, was a typical example. Her motivation for this side pilgrimage on her way to Rome was to see the Virgin Mary's veil, supposedly housed in the Assisi church. According to her own account, on entering and seeing the relic, "she wept, she sobbed, she cried" with great intensity and thereby obtained "grace, mercy, and forgiveness for herself, for all her friends, [and] for all her enemies."[64]

A Visit from Satan

Many shrines had other attractions for pilgrims besides relics. One of the most common claims to fame for religious shrines was a connection with miracles. One such miraculous event, for instance, occurred at an abbey in what was then northern France and is now Belgium. Supposedly, a monk was painting pictures of heaven and hell on the abbey's doors and, while in the midst of depicting the devil as an ugly creature, received a visit from Satan himself, who protested and demanded that his portrait show a handsome young man. The monk boldly refused and the furious Satan knocked away the scaffolding on which the man stood. As he fell, however, a nearby statue of the Virgin Mary suddenly came to life, stretched out her arms, and caught him, after which the devil retreated. In the decades and centuries following, pilgrims flocked to the abbey, now a sacred shrine, to see the statue of the Virgin and the monk's painting.

Saints and Heroes

The town of Santo Domingo de la Calzada in northern Spain also attained notoriety because of miracles. There, according to local legend, Saint Dominic's spirit brought back to life a young man who had been hanged for a crime he did not commit and also reanimated two birds that had already been killed and cooked. Visiting pilgrims came to see the saint's tomb and to feed local birds symbolizing those from the miracle. William Manchester describes another miracle, this one associated with England's Saint Germer's Abbey:

> Englishmen believed that the venerable abbot of St. Germer [who preached the Fourth Crusade in England] need only bless a fountain and lo! its waters would heal the sick, restore sight to the blind, and make the dumb speak. Once, according to pilgrims, the abbot had visited a

village parched for lack of water. He led the peasants into the church, and, as they watched, smote [struck] a stone with his staff. Behold! Water gushed forth, not only to slake [quench] thirsts but also possessing miraculous powers to cure all pain and illness.[65]

Other shrines derived their allure from their association with famous saints and heroes. For example, Assisi, which Margery Kempe so eagerly visited to see the Virgin's veil, drew just as many, if not more, pilgrims to see the location where Saint Francis lived and founded the Franciscan order. His chapel, his garden, and the room where he died were popular spots for prayer and personal meditation. Rocamadour in France was famous as the place where the hero Roland had made his own pilgrimage before going off to fight his last and most renowned battle for the glory of God. Just walking the grounds once trod by the legendary warrior were enough to fill the average pilgrim with genuine emotion and inspiration. Similarly, dozens of areas of Jerusalem and the Holy Land in Palestine attracted pilgrims who wanted to stand and kneel in the same locations frequented by Christ and his disciples.

A Crumbling Ruin Filled with Shrines

All of these attractions—sacred relics, miracles, and associations with religious figures and legendary heroes—drew pilgrims to the two most famous and often-visited Christian holy areas in Europe: Rome in Italy, and Compostela in Spain. These locations, along with Jerusalem, constituted the so-called grand tour of religious journeys in the Middle Ages. People believed that any pilgrim who

The serene church and convent of Assisi in central Italy, built on the site of Saint Francis's founding of the Franciscan Order.

managed to visit all three of these special holy places at least once earned penance that made up for almost any sin and also ensured a comfortable place in heaven.

In holiness and also in the sheer number of Christian shrines it housed, Rome was second only to Jerusalem and drew huge numbers of the faithful. According to some estimates, as many as five thousand people, most of them pilgrims, entered or left Rome each day. And during Lent, the city's peak season, a million or more souls crammed its streets, inns, and even its private homes, where renting rooms to pilgrims helped impoverished local residents make ends meet.

Having read and heard about how Rome had been the largest and grandest city of the ancient world, many pilgrims from faraway parts of Europe were more than a bit surprised at their first sight of the city. Indeed, what greeted them was a mere shadow, a pathetic remnant of the huge metropolis of glistening marble built by the first Roman emperor, Augustus Caesar, and his famous successors. According to Louise Collis, by the 1300s and 1400s

> Rome was a decayed city . . . and only half inhabited. Continually besieged by one side or another, the government having more or less broken down, most of the citizens had left. The town consisted of a network of narrow, dark . . . alleyways, broken occasionally by [public] squares,

on the flat tongue of land in [a] bend in the Tiber River. . . . As one went away from the river, towards the famous seven hills of ancient Rome, one found oneself passing into the country. Sheep and goats grazed among fallen columns and blocks from massive walls. Vineyards and orchards lined the famous streets which every educated person had heard of from the Latin [classical Roman] authors. The Forum [once the city's main square] made a convenient enclosure for oxen and pigs. . . . Sometimes, one came on clusters of houses, like villages in the fields. These had mostly been built with stone from a handy ruin, such as the [Colosseum], the temples of Jupiter, or Mercury.[66]

And yet, the fact that the city was mostly a crumbling ruin did not bother most pilgrims. They had come not to see the remains of its pagan, and therefore sinful, past, but to gaze on its many sacred Christian treasures and pray at its dozens of holy shrines. Collis writes:

Here were enshrined the memories and relics of the apostles and of innumerable martyrs who had endured horrible ends at pagan hands, by torture, execution, lynching, or being thrown as living fodder to the wild animals of the arena. At every turn were places where saints had been roasted, boiled or screwed to death. The details were all recounted [by tourist guides] to the accompaniment of pious screams of grief from the devout. Hostels were maintained for every nation. Careful guide books had been written, giving lists of churches, relics and the bloodthirsty martyr biographies [which described their gruesome deaths in graphic detail].[67]

Rome's Great Churches

Having read these guidebooks in advance, pilgrims eagerly sought out the shrines and relics they most wanted to see. There were more than three hundred churches to choose from, including the majestic cathedral of the Prince of the Apostles; Saint Lawrence's, where the martyrs Saint Stephen and Saint Lawrence were entombed; and Saint Peter's in Montorio, located on the spot where the apostle was crucified by the Romans. Each church had its unique attractions. At Santa Maria Maggiore's, for instance, one could see what was said to be the actual manger Christ rested in following his birth, the tombs of Saint Jerome and Saint Matthew, and a portrait of the Virgin Mary supposedly painted by Saint Luke. According to local tradition, for merely stepping into this church God forgave a pilgrim one-third of his or her sins. And in the ancient basilica of Saint John Lateran, the original residence of the popes, rested a wide array of supposed relics, including Saint Peter's and Saint Paul's heads, the ark of the covenant (the golden container that held the tablets of the Ten Commandments), and the bones and possessions of many saints.

The most renowned church of all, Saint Peter's Basilica, featured even more in the way of shrines, relics, and religious history and lore. First built in 330 and standing largely unchanged until the early 1500s (when it was remodeled and expanded), this massive edifice had, in addition to the saint's tomb, one hundred altars, seven major and ninety-three subsidiary. Pilgrims could also see and kiss what was said to be the rope Judas used to hang himself after betraying Christ and the stone on which Peter sat and wept after denying Christ. In addition, there was the chapel where, it was said, Peter sang his first mass, including the words "As often as you will thither come, seven thousand years you get pardon."[68] This meant that for praying at the shrine a pilgrim could expect to receive indulgence, or release from punishment for sin, for that many years.

Pilgrims received even more extravagant indulgences by viewing Saint Peter's most famous and precious relic, known variously as the Veronica and the Holy Vernicle. "This," explains Marjorie Rowling,

was the napkin on which an imprint of Christ's face appeared after St. Veronica had wiped the sweat from his brow on the way to Calvary. The mere sight of the Vernicle earned for the pilgrim a 12,000 years' indulgence—for the citizen of

Saint Peter's Basilica in Rome as it appears today (above), and the Basilica of Saint John Lateran, the original residence of the popes.

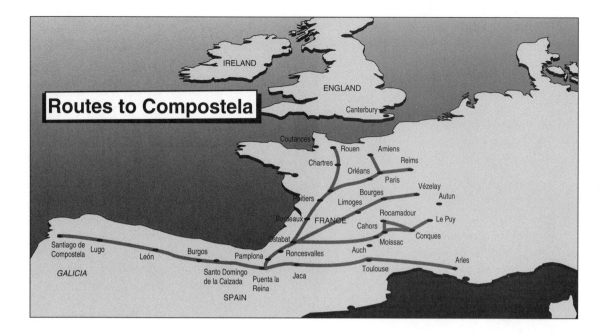

Routes to Compostela

IRELAND

ENGLAND

Canterbury

Coutances

Rouen   Amiens

Chartres   Reims

Orléans

Paris

Bourges   Vézelay

Poitiers   Autun

Limoges

Rocamadour

Bordeaux   FRANCE   Le Puy

Cahors

Ostabat   Conques

Moissac

Santiago de   Roncesvalles   Auch

Compostela   Lugo   Burgos   Pamplona   Arles

León   Toulouse

GALICIA   Santo Domingo   Jaca

de la Calzada   Puenta la

Reina

SPAIN

Rome [who did not have to make the sacrifice of a long journey to see the relic] this was reduced to a mere 3,000 years![69]

A Difficult but Worthwhile Journey

The other of continental Europe's two greatest religious attractions was the cathedral of Saint James at Santiago de Compostela, in Galicia in northern Spain. Trudging along long-established routes from England, Sweden, Denmark, Germany, Italy, Greece, and many other lands, at least half a million pilgrims a year converged onto the *camino francés*, the pilgrim road that ran through southern France southward toward Compostela. "Whether they traveled on foot (and some of the more devout barefoot)," the Winstons write,

> or rode on a donkey or horse, the pilgrims found it a long, weary ride all the

way across France to the Pyrenees [Mountains], then through the passes of the wild mountains and on across the whole of northern Spain almost to the Atlantic coast. The monks who maintained the hospices [along the way] had to provide straw for bedding and food and water for as many as came. The straw and food were home-grown, so that a productive monastery could afford to take care of sizable throngs of pilgrims. Charity required that the pilgrim be fed whether or not he could pay. Of course, nobles and rich merchants were expected to reimburse [pay back] the monastery by at least the amount they would have been charged at a commercial inn, or perhaps a bit more to help the monks succor [aid] the poor pilgrims.[70]

Most of the pilgrims who made this difficult journey claimed it was well worth the effort. Though Compostela was a small and unimportant-looking town situated seemingly

An Atmosphere of Serenity and Perfect Harmony

Its spires soaring some four hundred feet above the flatlands of Normandy in northern France, Mont-Saint-Michel was one of the most popular destinations for pilgrims in the Middle Ages. Located almost two kilometers off the French coast in the middle of a bay of the English Channel, the tiny three-acre island is completely surrounded by water twice a month, when the only way to reach it is by boat or a narrow earthen causeway built in 1879. In medieval times, pilgrims had to row or sail to Mont-Saint-Michel at high water. The island's one and very quaint cobblestone street winds in an ascending spiral to a magnificent Benedictine abbey, the original chapel of which Saint Aubert established in 708. According to Anne Fremantle in *Age of Faith*, "The chapel has long since vanished, but today's multilevel structure, built over [the course of] six centuries, runs the gamut of medieval architecture, from severe [simple and unadorned] early Romanesque to flamboyant [complex and highly decorated] Gothic."

Mont-Saint-Michel's principal allure for medieval pilgrims was the legend that Saint Aubert had built his chapel there at the direct command of the archangel Michael (in French, Saint Michel). Also, over the years many European kings and nobles donated buildings and relics to the abbey, helping to make it one of the top medieval tourist attractions. That popularity continued into modern times. An early-twentieth-century pilgrim, the American historian Henry Adams, commented in his 1913 book, *Mont-Saint-Michel and Chartres,* on the island's atmosphere of serenity and perfect harmony with nature. "Church and State," he wrote, "Soul and Body, God and Man, all are one at Mont-Saint-Michel."

The magnificent architecture of Mont-Saint-Michel creates a unique and stunning mirror image.

in the middle of nowhere, it happened to house one of the most sacred shrines in all Christendom. Michael Kuh summarizes the religious significance of the shrine:

> James, the Gospels [first four books of the New Testament] tell us, was one of the Galilean fishermen whom Christ turned into "fishers of men." He witnessed Christ's Transfiguration [transformation from human to spiritual form], and . . . became the first of the 12 apostles to suffer martyrdom. Tradition adds that James traveled widely, preached the Word [of Christ] throughout Roman Spain, finally returning to Jerusalem and death. Then in a miraculous seven-day voyage his disciples transported his body to Galicia, near present-day Santiago de Compostela.[71]

James's resting place was subsequently lost but then supposedly rediscovered in the ninth century. Soon after that, devout Christians built a cathedral on the spot and yearly pilgrimages began, culminating each year with great celebrations on July 25, what became the traditional Feast of Saint James.

The main ritual of the Compostela cathedral involved pilgrims' physically embracing a large statue of the saint located above the altar. Made of granite and painted in bright colors, it depicted James holding a pilgrim's staff in his left hand. Behind the altar and statue, wooden steps allowed the devout to climb up, place their hands on the image's shoulders, and kiss the gold-covered hood of its robe. After confessing to one of the priests on duty at all hours of the day and night, a pilgrim received a certificate documenting that he or she had actually worshiped at the shrine and so was eligible to wear the coveted Compostela badge shaped like a scallop shell. This

The triple spires of the cathedral at Santiago de Compostela, part of the magnificent shrine that drew thousands of the faithful each year during the Middle Ages.

badge, remarks Abelardo Moralejo, a former professor at the modern university in Compostela, "made men proud of themselves, of having physically reached a spiritual goal. Psychologically, this combination [of the physical and spiritual] produced the kind of [inspirational] motive most of us miss today."[72]

Compostela's Miraculous Legends

So inspirational was the Compostela shrine and its renowned pilgrimage, in fact, that many miraculous legends grew up surrounding it and its religious symbols. Today, people in the town still recall the story of a local horseman swept away by huge waves while riding along the shore on the way to his wedding. His grief-stricken bride appealed to Saint James and soon afterward the man rose from the sea, alive and covered with scallop shells.

Abbot Guibert told another, more famous miraculous tale about a man who went on pilgrimage to Compostela to do penance for the sin of fornication, or having sex outside of marriage. On the way, still carrying the sash of the woman he had sinned with, the man encountered the devil, who was disguised as Saint James himself. "Where are you going?" the false saint asked. "To St. James," the pilgrim replied. "I am that St. James to whom you are hastening," the devil declared. "Although up to now you have wallowed in the mire of the worst fornication, you now wish to appear a penitent, and you dare to present yourself before me . . . still girded with the belt of that foul whore of yours."

When the distraught pilgrim asked what he could do to gain forgiveness, his tormentor answered, "If you wish to bring forth fruit of repentance worthy of the shame you have wrought, for God's sake and mine cut off that member with which you have sinned—that is, your penis—and afterward take your very life, which you have led so evilly, by cutting your throat." That evening, the pilgrim did as the stern figure he thought to be Saint James had commanded. "Hearing the shriek of the dying man and the splash of the flowing blood, his companions awoke and . . . were grieved to see their comrade come to so dismal an end." After the funeral mass, however, thanks to the intervention of God, the Virgin Mary, and the real Saint James, the dead man suddenly and miraculously came back to life.[73]

In the Middle Ages, the existence of miracles was taken for granted and the authenticity of the vast majority of them was never questioned. Such magical and inspiring tales as those connected with Santiago de Compostela, St. Germer's Abbey, and other famous shrines magnified the individual reputations of these sites and at the same time added to the overall allure of holy pilgrimages. The miracles, the relics, the tombs of the saints, and the holy and historic grounds on which the sacred shrines rested all combined to attract Europe's legions of the devout. At these shrines, generations of men and women who were obsessed with sinning sought the forgiveness and salvation they heartily believed God would grant them. Abbot Guibert expressed this ever-present hope, saying, "Although I am forever sinning, compelled by my weakness . . . yet I in no wise lose the hope of amendment [improvement and salvation]."[74]

CHAPTER 6

The Ultimate Pilgrimage: Journey to Jerusalem, the Furnace of God

For Christians, the Holy Land in Palestine was, without question, the greatest tourist attraction of the Middle Ages. There, pilgrims visited the very places where Christ, his disciples, and other biblical figures lived, died, and, most importantly, performed various miracles and laid the groundwork for Christianity. Among the numerous "mustsee" sites in Palestine were Bethlehem, where Christ was born, and Nazareth, where he lived as a youth. Here was also the Jordan River, which the Israelites, after their exodus from Egypt, had crossed to enter the "promised land," and in which John the Baptist had baptized Christ, imparting to its waters what the devout believed were blessed properties. "The mere fact of having . . . dipped oneself in [the] Jordan," Louise Collis remarks, "was sufficient to assure a man of a straight passage to heaven when the time came."[75]

Above all, the Holy Land featured Jerusalem, where Christ had been crucified and buried and, according to the Gospels, had risen from the dead on the third day after the Crucifixion. Over the years, the faithful had erected a church and huge stone enclosure around the Holy Sepulcher, the rocky tomb where his body was said to have rested before his resurrection, and this monument alone was enough to draw pilgrims from all around the Mediterranean world. In the eleventh century, wrote the Christian chronicler Bernard of

Saint Michael's Mount, "began to flow towards the Holy Sepulcher so great a multitude as, ere this, no man could have hoped for. First of all went the meaner [poorer] folk, then men of middle rank, and, lastly, very many kings and counts, marchises, and bishops."[76]

One reason for visiting the Holy Land, of course, was to seek both forgiveness for one's sins and salvation. After all, people reasoned, if the infamous Count Fulk of Anjou, after committing so many terrible crimes, could gain pardon by journeying to Jerusalem, more righteous pilgrims who made the trip would surely earn a place in heaven. Another motivation for the pilgrimage to the Holy Land was to strengthen one's faith and ties to God, to seek the "truth" about God and his relationship with human beings. Abbot Guibert described a man who was unsure about his religious beliefs and worshiped many "false" gods until he went to the Holy Land, where he declared:

> At last I reached the settled conviction that . . . the unique creation and rule of one God could exist, and that as all things come from Him alone, so He . . . holds the universe together, and that this ought to be believed. After my mind had become fixed upon one God, and I had scornfully rejected the temples [of the false gods] and their idols forever, my heart seemed to be cleansed from the filth of idolatry,

and the celestial purity of the unique true religion shone forth in it.[77]

Venice and Departure

In order to get to the Holy Land and its sacred sites, pilgrims first had to reach Venice, in northeastern Italy, the main point of departure for ships heading to Palestine. This meant that nearly all European pilgrims had to cross the "roof of Europe," the towering and treacherous peaks of the Alps, which formed a wide and mighty barrier across the northern edge of the Italian boot. As Collis reports, the Alpine crossing Margery Kempe and William Weaver made in the early 1400s illustrates the difficulty of the journey and the extreme determination of the devout to reach the Holy Land:

> They crept along the precipitous [steep] paths together. The wind must have been piercingly cold, the mountains covered with snow. On some days, perhaps, there were blizzards, or icy rain, or mist. Darkness came down early, and if they lost the way, they might fall over a cliff, or simply freeze to death in this desolate robber country. There were certain pilgrim hymns sung particularly at bad moments to keep the spirits up and call God's attention to his servants' need. . . . They were following the Inn valley into the heart of the Alps. Finally, they came to Resia, where it was necessary to cross over

Groups of pilgrims tour the massive stone enclosures of Jerusalem's Church of the Holy Sepulcher, built on the site of Christ's tomb.

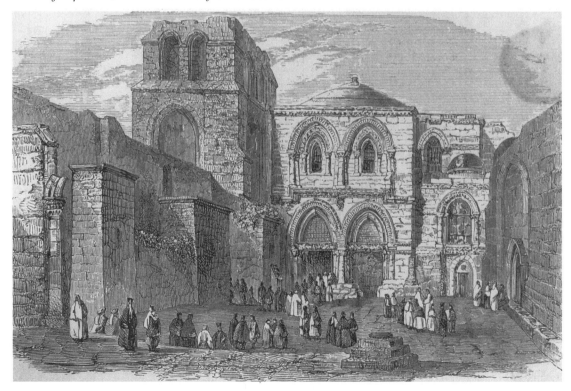

A Renaissance depiction of Venice, the city of a thousand canals, as it appeared in 1338.

the pass (4944 feet) to the valley of the Adige. The long descent began from here, through ravines, past cascades and overhanging rocks. The scenery was magnificent, but the fifteenth century romantic fancy did not dwell on landscape [but rather on God and holy topics]. It must have been a great moment when they sighted Bolzano [about eighty miles northwest of Venice], chief center of trade between Venice and the north.[78]

Once they arrived in Venice, pilgrims first rested after their long overland journeys and then visited the many shrines and relics the city featured. Guides with special licenses issued by the local government helped pilgrims find their way around, secure lodgings, change money, and shop for provisions they would need for the last leg of the journey to the Holy Land.

Eventually, the time came to book passage on outgoing ships. Sailings usually occurred twice each year, in the spring and fall, at which times city officials raised special banners in the central public square, the Piazza San Marco. There, ship captains, who also had to have state-issued licenses, signed up both crews and groups of pilgrims. On average, a ticket to the Holy Land in the fourteenth century cost about eight or nine pounds (or livres, units of currency then roughly standard in France, England, and many other parts of Europe), the approximate cost of buying a horse, a major investment for all but the well-to-do. This price included all meals, inn charges, entrance fees, tourist guide fees, and other costs on the round trip.

Many pilgrims learned the hard way the importance of negotiating with ship captains in advance regarding matters ranging from everyday comforts to unexpected and unfortunate circumstances, such as dying on the voyage. Pilgrims were advised to insert special clauses in their contracts, Collis explains,

The Foundation of the World

One of the shrines that the Muslims who controlled Jerusalem would not allow visiting medieval Christian pilgrims to see was the Dome of the Rock, also called the Mosque of Omar. This Muslim holy building had been erected by Caliph Omar shortly after a Muslim army captured the city in 638. The mosque rose on the site of the old Jewish Temple of Solomon, destroyed by the Babylonians in 587 B.C. and later rebuilt as the Second Temple, only to be leveled once again in A.D. 70, this time by the Romans when Palestine was part of their vast empire. Within the mosque rested the Shetiyyah, *the sacred rock thought by the ancient Jews to be the "foundation stone" on which God had built the rest of the world. On this stone Solomon had placed the ark of the covenant, the container holding the tablets of the Ten Commandments, which Jews, Christians, and Muslims alike believed God had given to Israel through the prophet Moses. The Muslims held that the sacred stone marked the spot from which the prophet Muhammad ascended into heaven. In this excerpt from his book* The Sign and the Seal, *scholar Graham Hancock describes the still-surviving Dome of the Rock, which he visited in 1990.*

"A large and elegant octagonal building faced with rich blue tiling, its dominant exterior feature was its massive golden dome. . . . The interior of the building . . . quite literally took my breath away. The soaring ceiling, the columns and arches supporting the inner octagon, the various niches and recesses, the mosaics [pictures formed of small tiles], the inscriptions—all these elements and many more melded together in a sublime harmony of proportion and design that gave eloquent expression to humanity's yearning for the divine. . . . As though attracted by some powerful magnetic force, I felt my attention tugged down . . . towards the very center of the mosque where a huge tawny rock perhaps thirty feet across . . . lay directly beneath the dome. This was the *Shetiyyah* and, as I approached it, I was aware that my heart was beating more quickly than usual. . . . I stood there, lost in my own thoughts, drinking in through the pores of my fingers the immense antiquity [age] of this strange and wonderful stone."

so that "if the worst happened and one died, one's belongings [would not] be seized from those to whom one had willed them. Also, a proportion of the passage money ought to be returned."[79] And English traveler William Wey, a veteran of two Jerusalem pilgrimages, advised in his *Itineraries:*

Be sure if you go in a galley to choose a place on the upper stage [hold], for in the lowest it is right smoldering hot and stinking. And you shall pay for your galley and for your meat and drink to Jaffa [Jerusalem's port town], and back again to Venice, 40 ducats [common European gold coins of varying values] to be in a good, honest place, where you will be comfortable and properly looked after. But take care to make your covenant [contract] with your patron [captain] before the duke and other lords of Venice [that is, have it witnessed], under surety of 100 ducats. This includes stopping at certain harbors on the way to get fresh water, bread and meat.[80]

Advice from Veteran Pilgrims

After the ships finally launched and headed over the waves toward the east, the pilgrims faced many days of idleness as well as confined, miserable conditions. To help pass the time, they often spent hours poring over guidebooks, purchased in Venice, that gave advice about what to look for and how to conduct themselves in the Holy Land. Wey's *Itineraries*, one of the more popular of these books, gave the following advice about what to do when arriving at various interim ports as well as at Jaffa:

> When you come to haven towns [those catering to pilgrims and travelers], if you shall tarry [stay] there three days, go [immediately] to land to secure lodging ahead of the others, for it will be taken quickly, and, if there is any good food, get it before the others arrive. On arriving at Jaffa, the port of Jerusalem, the same haste must be observed so as to secure one of the best asses. You shall pay no more for the best than for the worst.[81]

Another book, Pero Tafur's *Travels*, told pilgrims more about what to expect upon arrival at Jaffa. A Franciscan monastery, named Mount Sion, he said, existed near Jerusalem and the prior, or head monk, was most helpful to visiting Christians, who otherwise would be completely at the mercy of the local Muslims, who would grasp any opportunity to take advantage of them. The Saracens, the name Christians used to describe all Muslims at the time, required that the pilgrims get a letter of "safe conduct" from the local sultan, or Saracen governor. Otherwise, the locals could and would take no responsibility for the safety of Christian visitors. It was common knowledge that pilgrims, and Westerners in general, who had no signed safe conduct letter faced a strong probability of being robbed and/or murdered while in Palestine. Hearing of the arrival of a new pilgrim ship, Tafur wrote, the prior of Mount Sion "sends two of his friars to the Governor of Jerusalem who return with the Sultan's safe conduct. The pilgrims then go ashore and deliver their names in writing for the Governor's use while the friars retain one [copy] for themselves."[82]

The guidebooks were bursting with other tidbits of advice for the traveler. First, one should make sure to bring a cushion, which would help to soften the impact of long donkey rides and of sitting on wood or stone for extended periods during tours of the ancient shrines. One should also take along some wine, for the Saracens, the books warned, did not drink and only a few scattered Christian trading posts had wine supplies. And always have plenty of water when entering one of the many stretches of desert in the region. In addition, the books offered much advice about relations with the local Saracens, beginning with the warning to avoid talking about religion, for this would invariably lead to a heated argument and, very likely, to violence. Also, under no circumstances make passes at their women; try not to stand too close to them, since they might pick your pocket; do not stray from your escorted party because you might get lost and then be at their mercy; speak kindly to them, even though you despise them, in order to stay on their good side, for they control the area and without their cooperation seeing the holy places is impossible. "Remember always," went the refrain of guidebooks and local Christian friars alike, "that all [Saracens] are dishonest and also all Jews and eastern Christians. Such people simply have no conscience, especially the last."[83]

A Miserable Stay at Jaffa

Eventually, the ships approached the shores of the Holy Land, a sight that brought tears to the eyes of many pilgrims. At last, the great spiritual adventure they had dreamed of for so long was at hand. But the first chapter of this adventure proved both difficult and disheartening. After disembarking, the travelers had to line up and, just as described in Tafur's book, one by one give their names to the local Saracen official. This was no easy process, for the Saracens usually had a hard time pronouncing what were for them strange-sounding European names. Then, while awaiting their safe conduct from the sultan, which might take a few days, the pilgrims were forced to bed down in some caverns along the shore, known as Saint Peter's Caves. The name was probably coined by some of the first pilgrims who stayed in these miserable holes, who in their ordeal fancied themselves martyrs on a par with that revered saint. "Dripping with damp and decay," explains Collis, these stone vaults

> were ordinarily used by animals. The smell was frightful, even to people accustomed to the communal cabin on the ship. There was nothing for [them to do] but to shovel the dung into a corner and reflect on those

European pilgrims hand over tribute to local Saracens, part of the toll that had to be paid for the privilege of visiting the Holy Land.

passages in the scriptures describing the great benefits to be obtained from lodging humbly on a dunghill—the story of Job, for instance, who had actually lived in this city for a period, it was said.[84]

Adding to the misery of a stay in the caves, the local Saracens took advantage of the pilgrims' predicament. Gangs of armed men sometimes showed up and demanded a penny from each pilgrim, supposedly the fee for lodging there but really just a bribe extorted under threat of harm. Since the pilgrims' safe conduct had not yet arrived, the local Saracen officials held that the visitors were not yet under their protection and turned their backs, leaving no choice but to pay up. Another tactic local ruffians used to obtain even more illegal money was to bait the Christians into violent confrontation. They tripped them, grabbed at their clothes, and told obscene jokes, all in an attempt to provoke a fight. If a pilgrim took the bait and assaulted a Saracen, he or she was subject to immediate arrest, often followed by imprisonment and torture, and the only way to escape this fate was a generous payoff to those who had started the trouble in the first place. Needless to say, rather than risk such trouble, most pilgrims bit their tongues and endured the harassment.

When the safe conduct finally arrived and the journey to Jerusalem began, the pilgrims breathed a hearty sigh of relief. "We therefore arose with joy," wrote Felix Fabri, a pilgrim who visited the Holy Land in the 1400s, "and came forth from our prison, even as captives do from the place of their captivity."[85] After the baggage had been loaded onto donkeys, the visitors and their hosts struck out for the holy city, about thirty-nine miles away across rugged, arid territory. The typical caravan consisted of about two hundred pilgrims; the Mount Sion prior, his servants, and some of his friars; the ship captains and perhaps a few of his crewmen; the local Saracen officials, now responsible for the visitors' safety; and a column of soldiers provided by the sultan to fend off possible attacks by Arab bandits, who lurked in the barren hills.

The journey, though relatively short, was slow paced and usually took at least two days. It was common to spend the night at the village of Ramleh, where the pilgrims had to sleep either in a local Saracen inn, which served Saracens first and was often full, or in the marketplace. To help remedy these conditions, in the fifteenth century England's duke of Burgundy generously built a pilgrim hospice in Ramleh. No matter what the conditions, however, once the journey was under way the pilgrims had to do what they were told and follow their guides at all times. "Their board and lodging, outings, tours, guides, devotions and whole timetable were strictly arranged," Collis writes. "There were hundreds of sites to be visited and all had to be seen in three weeks at the most, after which the travelers were delivered again to their ships and sent home."[86]

Christendom's Most Sacred Spots

The first and most eagerly anticipated of these sites, of course, was Jerusalem, holiest of all Christian cities. History and spiritual inspirations abounded here, on the streets and in the buildings once frequented by biblical figures and saints. Among the many attractions was the so-called Pillar of Pilate (in reference to Pontius Pilate, the Roman governor in charge of Jerusalem at the time of Christ's death), the post to which Christ had been bound for whipping before the

The holy city of Jerusalem, with its huge and ancient defensive walls, looms at last before expectant travelers who have journeyed from afar to see it.

Crucifixion. Some pilgrims, conditioned since childhood with horrific stories about Christ's sufferings, were overcome with emotion at the mere sight of the pillar. A surviving chronicle describes the reaction of an eleventh-century visitor, Richard, abbot of Saint Vannes:

> When he gazed on the Pillar of Pilate . . . and relived the binding and the scourging [whipping] of the Savior, the spitting, the smiting [punching], the mocking, the crown of thorns; when . . . he beheld in his mind the Savior crucified, pierced with a lance, mocked by the passers-by, crying out with a loud voice and surrendering His spirit, when he, Richard, relived these scenes, what heartfelt pain,

what bitterness of tears do you think sprang from the pangs of such remembrance?[87]

Many pilgrims registered similar emotional reactions to other holy places and objects in Jerusalem. One could see the site of the Last Supper of Christ and his disciples; the preaching stone on which, it was claimed, he had stood while speaking to the multitudes; and the hill on which he had delivered the famous Sermon on the Mount. So many sacred spots existed so close to one another that pilgrims could be seen stepping twenty paces in one direction and ten in another to locate the next attraction. One of the most popular guidebooks of the Late Middle Ages, John Poloner's *Description of the Holy Land*, contained detailed instructions on how many paces to step in order to find the holy spots. "I counted with the greatest care I could," declared Poloner in his preface. Typical of his instructions were those leading a pilgrim away from the preaching stone: "Twelve feet from this inscribed stone there is another stone fixed in the ground on the place where the Blessed Virgin Mary sat and listened to her Son's preaching. Also, five paces off, is the place where her cottage stood, wherein she dwelt after her Son's Ascension."[88]

By far the main attraction for pilgrims visiting Jerusalem was the stone enclosure of the Church of the Holy Sepulcher (also called the Church of the Resurrection), which housed the most sacred spots and objects in all of Christendom. Outside in front of the church stretched a wide courtyard covered with white stones of highly pol-

ished marble. Here, even before they had reached the long-anticipated inner sanctum, some pilgrims lost all control and collapsed sobbing or engaged in some other kind of emotional display. As Seigneur D'Anglure, a pilgrim of the 1390s, described the scene, "We flung ourselves down . . . and prayed and kissed the earth many times." Some visitors sprawled "powerless on the ground, forsaken by their strength," while others walked aimlessly around the courtyard "beating their breasts as though they were driven by an evil spirit." Still others kneeled down and "prayed with tears, holding their arms out in the form of a cross."[89]

Then the pilgrims entered the holy enclosure. A group of dignified-looking Saracens stood at the gate to collect entry fees and also to check the pilgrims' names against the master lists compiled on the beaches at

Two of Christianity's most sacred events: the Last Supper (left), and the Sermon on the Mount. Pilgrims eagerly sought out the sites of both.

Christian pilgrims pay a fee to Saracen officials who stand guard outside of the Church of the Holy Sepulcher.

Jaffa. Franciscan friars acted as guides, each escorting a small group of pilgrims around the shrine and identifying and explaining the sites and relics. These friars first gave the visitors a little lecture, warning about the expected rules of behavior in the enclosure. Chipping or carving of the holy relics, for instance, was not allowed, nor was pushing or shoving one's neighbors in an effort to be first at each sacred spot.

Once these preliminaries were out of the way, the groups began their tour, which typically went on for many hours. The visitors, bearing candles, saw the place where Christ had appeared as a gardener to Mary Magdalene, the prison in which he had languished after being condemned, the spot on which the Roman soldiers had gambled for his robe, and the stone on which he had sat after being

crowned with thorns. Eventually, the pilgrims arrived at the holiest of holies, the most revered spot in all Christendom—the mound of Calvary, where the true cross had stood. Many onlookers, even some of those who up to this point had been able to maintain their composure, now broke down and surrendered to a flood of emotion. Margery Kempe's reaction was particularly dramatic. "For years," Collis writes,

> she had dwelt on Christ's suffering on the cross, turning it backwards and forwards in her imagination, finding emotional satisfaction in the grisly details of the scene. This was perfectly usual in the Middle Ages, as were the howls and tears of piety. . . . But now, she experienced something altogether more intense, which sur-

prised onlookers by its violence, even though it happened in the middle of a crowd of excited devotees. Holding out her arms in the form of a cross, she fell on the ground in convulsions. . . . Extraordinary screams broke from her.[90]

Kempe was not the only pilgrim overcome by the experience. While she writhed and moaned, visiting priests and monks argued loudly over which of them should have the honor of saying mass inside the sacred enclosure. Occasionally such squabbles erupted into fistfights.

Memories to Cherish

Once they had seen the Holy Sepulcher, pilgrims spent the next couple of weeks touring other interesting attractions. A few, perhaps out of curiosity, desired to see the inside of Muslim mosques, which the local Saracens forbade. In 1437, Pero Tafur bribed a local man, who smuggled him into the Mosque of Omar (the famed Dome of the Rock) at the risk of both of their lives. "At one o'clock in the night I entered," Tafur later wrote, "dressed in his clothes. . . . If I had been recognized there, I should have been killed immediately."[91]

Most other pilgrims preferred to stick with touring recognized Christian shrines, of which there were more than enough to occupy the remainder of their stay. Most made the side trip to Bethlehem, located about five miles south of Jerusalem. There, a

church, the Nativity of Saint Mary, housed most of the sites and relics associated with Christ's birth, including, supposedly, the very spot where Mary had delivered him. In an underground vault below the church, pilgrims viewed what was said to be a miraculous portrait of Saint Jerome, who had once lived in the building while translating the Scriptures into Latin. According to Felix Fabri's account, "If carefully and minutely looked at, there appears in it the figure of an old bearded man, lying on his back on a mat, in the dress of a dead monk and beside him the figure of a lion. This picture is not produced by art, or work, but by simple polishing alone."[92]

After numerous other side trips to locales such as the Mount of Olives; the tomb of Lazarus, whom, the devout believed, Christ had raised from the dead; and Mary Magdalene's house, the pilgrims returned to Jaffa and the ships waiting to take them home. It had been an exhausting but enlightening journey, one whose memories they would cherish for the rest of their lives. They had made the ultimate pilgrimage for their own salvation and for the glory of the Lord, "whose fire," the Bible stated, "is in Zion [or Sion, a sacred mound in Jerusalem], and whose furnace is in Jerusalem . . . and he will be the stability of our times, [giving people an] abundance of salvation, wisdom, and knowledge."[93] To the medieval mind, so deeply conditioned by faith, such words were more than enough to live by. And happily to die for.

A Modern March Through History

The idea and practice of holy pilgrimage did not die out as the Middle Ages gave way to the modern world. Indeed, many of the sites visited by medieval pilgrims remain the holiest shrines in the Christian world and continue yearly to attract large numbers of the faithful. That such journeys still excite and inspire these eager travelers is illustrated in the words of a French priest, Père Georges, who in the 1960s made the trek to Compostela along the same road, the *camino francés*, used by pilgrims for nearly a thousand years:

> This has been the dream of my entire life. Twenty-nine days I have walked from Poitiers [in France], never leaving the path of my predecessor Picaud [a twelfth-century clergyman from Poitiers]. I cannot express . . . the joy this has given me, this journey of faith and tradition. I have been freezing and sunstruck, exhausted, hungry—all these extremes from which today we are protected. I have been given kindness and hospitality everywhere. For me these 29 days have been a march through history and brotherhood that I shall never forget.[94]

Georges was but one of many thousands of pilgrims who continue to march across northern Spain, climb the steps behind the huge statue of the saint, hug its gold-plated robe, and whisper into its ear *"Merci Saint Jacques* [thank you, Saint James]."

As it was in the medieval age, when faith so sharply defined the European mind, the road to Compostela is still littered with tales of miracles. In the late 1960s, in Rocamadour, France, traditionally one of the most important stops on the pilgrim way, a guide working at the Chapel of Sainte Marie told the story of an English traveler who had passed through a few years before:

> This Englishwoman, about 30, had advanced tuberculosis in her left leg. She could barely hobble. Doctors had done her no good. Here she prayed for a cure. And she walked out of this chapel as well as you or I. The cure has lasted. She returns every year to give thanks.[95]

Today's Shrines

Pilgrimage, prayer, and a belief in miracles remain important factors in the continuing worship and tourist trade at many other holy cities. Rome regularly draws hundreds of thousands of pilgrims from around the world, flocking to view the massive basilica of Saint Peter and to receive blessings from the pope. And many of these travelers still make the same side trip Margery Kempe did so long ago, northward through the rugged Apennine Mountains to the town of Assisi. There, they meditate, just as she did, at the basilica of Saint Francis, a building begun in 1228 on

*Pope John Paul II greets a crowd of modern-day pilgrims from his balcony at
Saint Peter's Basilica.*

the day after the poor, devout friar was canonized. British scholar James Harpur describes how Assisi today survives nearly unchanged, a living time capsule of the medieval era from which it sprang and a monument to the saint whose simple piety and faith so inspired the medieval mind:

No other town in Italy, perhaps no other town in the world, is quite like Assisi. At every step, the traveler is reminded of St. Francis . . . the poor man of God. Yet Assisi does not look particularly striking from a distance. It is one among many such hilltop towns in this beautiful region. But the visitor only has to share for a few days the frugal life of one of Assisi's convents or monasteries, climb its narrow medieval streets . . . or light a candle in one of its churches to feel that it would be possible at any moment at the turn of a street to come face to face with the saint himself.[96]

Jerusalem and the Holy Land in Palestine remain the main attractions for today's Christian pilgrims. Now controlled by the modern State of Israel and with a population about 75 percent Jewish and 20 percent Arab, Jerusalem still boasts tourism as its number one industry. And, along with many other sacred sites in Palestine, the city continues to be holy to all three religions—Judaism, Christianity, and Islam. For visiting Christians, the Holy Sepulcher holds the same allure it did for medieval pilgrims like Felix Fabri, Pero Tafur, and Margery Kempe. Magnificent and solemn ceremonies take place in and around the sacred enclosure each year in the Easter season, beginning with a procession through the city streets on Palm Sunday. For Jewish pilgrims, the main attraction is the Wailing Wall, the only remaining section of the original Temple of Solomon, located in a section known as the Old City. Muslim pilgrims are drawn to the Dome of the Rock, the mosque housing the stone on which, they believe, the prophet Muhammad stood prior to his ascension into heaven.

Leaving Jerusalem, modern Christian pilgrims follow in the footsteps of their medieval predecessors and visit other sacred Palestinian sites, including the Church of the Nativity in Bethlehem. At the town of Hebron, south of Bethlehem, they enter caves said to hold the tombs of biblical figures, including Abraham, Sarah, Isaac, and Jacob. In northern Israel, pilgrims visit Nazareth, where Christ lived as a boy, and then travel a few miles northeast to the fabled Sea of Galilee to stand on the spot

A group of Roman Catholic nuns, bearing traditional palm leaves, march across the historic Mount of Olives toward Old Jerusalem.

where, according to tradition, as a young man he fed five thousand people with only five loaves of bread and two fish.

Pilgrims Old and New

The difference between such modern pilgrimages and those of old lies neither in the holiness of the shrines nor in the piety and sincerity of the thousands of faithful who visit them each year. What *has* changed significantly since medieval days is the strength of the church's hold over society as a whole. Once, virtually every person in Western society was a Christian who recognized the authority of the pope in Italy. Today, in addition to such Roman Catholics, Christianity is divided into many Protestant and other sects who do not recognize the spiritual leadership of the pope and who worship God in their own diverse ways.

Also, society has become much more secularized, or worldly. Through the artistic Renaissance, age of exploration, and scientific revolution, all of which reshaped the world in early modern times, the medieval mind, too,

was reshaped. For most people, strict adherence to religious ideas and rules gave way to a reliance on self, scientific principles, and civil authorities. Though most Christians still believe in God and many go to church on a regular basis, only a minority still exhibit the degree of faith and dedication that motivates the act of pilgrimage to a distant shrine.

Yet those who do make the effort say that they are never disappointed. For a brief moment they turn away from the noisy hustle and bustle of today's technological world and experience a touch of the simpler, quieter, and more godly vision that inspired their medieval ancestors. For the devout pilgrim, old or new, life's prime motivating force was and still is the honor of God, expressed nowhere more perfectly than in this prayer by Saint Francis:

> Let us have in our hearts, let us love, adore, serve . . . praise . . . [and] glorify God. He is without beginning and without end . . . glorious, exalted, sublime, most high, sweet, lovely . . . and always worthy of being desired above all things, in all the ages of ages. Amen.[97]

Notes

Introduction: A Civilization Obsessed with God

1. Quoted in Edith Rickert et al., eds., *Chaucer's World*. New York: Columbia University Press, 1948, pp. 260–61.
2. Quoted in Marjorie Rowling, *Life in Medieval Times*. New York: Berkley Publishing, 1968, pp. 95–96.
3. William Manchester, *A World Lit Only by Fire: The Medieval Mind and the Renaissance*. Boston: Little, Brown, 1992, p. 64.
4. Clara Winston and Richard Winston, *Daily Life in the Middle Ages*. New York: American Heritage, 1975, p. 97.
5. Charles Van Doren, *A History of Knowledge: Past, Present, and Future*. New York: Ballantine Books, 1991, p. 100.

Chapter 1: The City of God: How Faith Shaped and Inspired the Medieval Mind

6. Anne Fremantle, *Age of Faith*. New York: Time, Inc., 1965, p. 12.
7. Quoted in Fremantle, *Age of Faith*, p. 14.
8. Quoted in Frederick B. Artz, *The Mind of the Middle Ages, A.D. 200–1500: An Historical Survey*. New York: Knopf, 1954, p. 179.
9. Quoted in Artz, *The Mind of the Middle Ages*, p. 180.
10. Henri Pirenne, *Medieval Cities: Their Origins and the Revival of Trade*. New York: Doubleday, 1956, p. 5.
11. Quoted in Manchester, *A World Lit Only by Fire*, p. 10.
12. Winstons, *Daily Life*, p. 47.

13. Fremantle, *Age of Faith*, p. 21.
14. Quoted in Fremantle, *Age of Faith*, p. 16.
15. Louise Collis, *Memoirs of a Medieval Woman: The Life and Times of Margery Kempe*. New York: Harper and Row, 1964, p. 11.
16. John F. Benton, ed., *Self and Society in Medieval France: The Memoirs of Abbot Guibert of Nogent*. Translated by C. C. S. Bland. New York: Harper and Row, 1970, p. 121.

Chapter 2: To See What Lay Beyond the Horizon: The Pilgrims and Their Motives

17. Gertrude Hartman, *Medieval Days and Ways*. New York: Macmillan, 1960, pp. 162–63.
18. J. J. Bagley, *Life in Medieval England*. New York: G. P. Putnam's Sons, 1960, p. 84.
19. Geoffrey Chaucer, *The Canterbury Tales*. Translated by J. U. Nicolson. Vol. 22 of *Great Books of the Western World*. Chicago: Encyclopaedia Britannica, 1952, p. 162.
20. Quoted in Eileen Power, *Medieval People*. New York: Barnes and Noble, 1963, p. 94.
21. Chaucer, *Canterbury Tales*, p. 258.
22. Chaucer, *Canterbury Tales*, p. 161.
23. Power, *Medieval People*, p. 81.
24. Winstons, *Daily Life*, p. 73.
25. Collis, *Memoirs of a Medieval Woman*, p. 44.
26. Quoted in Rowling, *Life in Medieval Times*, p. 72.

27. Quoted in Rowling, *Life in Medieval Times*, pp. 72–73.

28. Quoted in Rowling, *Life in Medieval Times*, pp. 78–79.

29. Collis, *Memoirs of a Medieval Woman*, p. 62.

30. Quoted in Rowling, *Life in Medieval Times*, p. 94.

31. Manchester, *A World Lit Only by Fire*, p. 59.

32. Chaucer, *Canterbury Tales*, p. 168.

Chapter 3: "How Far Is It from Here to Paris?" The Rules of a Successful Pilgrimage

33. Quoted in Rickert, *Chaucer's World*, p. 283.

34. Collis, *Memoirs of a Medieval Woman*, p. 53.

35. Quoted in Dorothy Mills, *The Middle Ages*. New York: G. P. Putnam's Sons, 1935, pp. 234–35.

36. Quoted in Rickert, *Chaucer's World*, p. 269.

37. Quoted in Rickert, *Chaucer's World*, p. 267.

38. Quoted in Rickert, *Chaucer's World*, p. 267.

39. Barbara W. Tuchman, *A Distant Mirror: The Calamitous 14th Century*. New York: Knopf, 1978, p. 57.

40. Quoted in Fremantle, *Age of Faith*, p. 122.

41. William S. Davis, *Life on a Medieval Barony*. New York: Harper and Row, 1951, pp. 297–98.

42. Quoted in Rickert, *Chaucer's World*, p. 269.

43. Quoted in Georges Duby, ed., "Revelations of the Medieval World," in *A History of Private Life*, Vol. 2. Cambridge, MA: Harvard University Press, 1988, pp. 255–56.

44. Quoted in Rickert, *Chaucer's World*, pp. 278–80.

45. Chaucer, *Canterbury Tales*, p. 234.

46. Collis, *Memoirs of a Medieval Woman*, p. 55.

Chapter 4: Medieval Mishaps and Mayhem: When Pilgrimages Went Wrong

47. Quoted in Rickert, *Chaucer's World*, p. 13.

48. Collis, *Memoirs of a Medieval Woman*, p. 71.

49. Quoted in Philippe Braunstein, "Toward Intimacy: The Fourteenth and Fifteenth Centuries," in *A History of Private Life* Vol. 2, pp. 587–88.

50. Quoted in Rickert, *Chaucer's World*, p. 257.

51. Quoted in Rickert, *Chaucer's World*, p. 257.

52. Quoted in Benton, *Self and Society in Medieval France*, pp. 194–95.

53. Winstons, *Daily Life*, p. 115.

54. Quoted in Rickert, *Chaucer's World*, p. 269.

55. Quoted in Rowling, *Life in Medieval Times*, p. 187.

56. Quoted in Otto Friedrich, *The End of the World: A History*. New York: Fromm International, 1986, p. 117.

57. Quoted in Friedrich, *The End of the World*, p. 116.

58. Quoted in Friedrich, *The End of the World*, p. 126.

59. Quoted in Fremantle, *Age of Faith*, p. 63.

Chapter 5: Reaching a Spiritual Goal: Europe's Many Sacred Shrines and Relics

60. Quoted in Rickert, *Chaucer's World*, p. 262.

61. Quoted in Merle Severy, ed., *The Age of Chivalry*. Washington, DC: National Geographic Society, 1969, p. 178.

62. Quoted in Rickert, *Chaucer's World*, p. 390.

63. Davis, *Life on a Medieval Barony*, p. 307.

64. Quoted in Collis, *Memoirs of a Medieval Woman*, p. 122.

65. Manchester, *A World Lit Only by Fire*, p. 63.

66. Collis, *Memoirs of a Medieval Woman*, p. 128.

67. Collis, *Memoirs of a Medieval Woman*, p. 129.

68. Quoted in Rowling, *Life in Medieval Times*, p. 104.

69. Rowling, *Life in Medieval Times*, p. 104.

70. Winstons, *Daily Life*, p. 74.

71. Quoted in Severy, *The Age of Chivalry*, p. 175.

72. Quoted in Severy, *The Age of Chivalry*, p. 177.

73. Quoted in Benton, *Self and Society in Medieval France*, pp. 218–20.

74. Quoted in Benton, *Self and Society in Medieval France*, p. 86.

Chapter 6: The Ultimate Pilgrimage: Journey to Jerusalem, the Furnace of God

75. Collis, *Memoirs of a Medieval Woman*, p. 51.

76. Quoted in Mills, *The Middle Ages*, pp. 180–81.

77. Quoted in Benton, *Self and Society in Medieval France*, p. 123.

78. Collis, *Memoirs of a Medieval Woman*, pp. 61–62.

79. Collis, *Memoirs of a Medieval Woman*, p. 72.

80. Quoted in Rowling, *Life in Medieval Times*, p. 96.

81. Quoted in Rowling, *Life in Medieval Times*, p. 99.

82. Quoted in Rowling, *Life in Medieval Times*, p. 99.

83. Collis, *Memoirs of a Medieval Woman*, pp. 87–88.

84. Collis, *Memoirs of a Medieval Woman*, p. 82.

85. Quoted in Collis, *Memoirs of a Medieval Woman*, p. 85.

86. Collis, *Memoirs of a Medieval Woman*, p. 52.

87. Quoted in Rowling, *Life in Medieval Times*, p. 101.

88. Quoted in Collis, *Memoirs of a Medieval Woman*, p. 94.

89. Quoted in Collis, *Memoirs of a Medieval Woman*, p. 92.

90. Collis, *Memoirs of a Medieval Woman*, p. 100.

91. Quoted in Rowling, *Life in Medieval Times*, p. 100.

92. Quoted in Collis, *Memoirs of a Medieval Woman*, p. 106.

93. Isa. 31:9 and 33:6.

Conclusion: A Modern March Through History

94. Quoted in Severy, *The Age of Chivalry*, pp. 194–95.

95. Quoted in Severy, *The Age of Chivalry*, p. 182.

96. James Harpur and Jennifer Westwood, *The Atlas of Legendary Places*. New York: Weidenfeld and Nicolson, 1989, p. 158.

97. Quoted in Norman F. Cantor, ed., *The Medieval World: 300–1300*. New York: Macmillan, 1963, p. 269.

For Further Reading

Timothy Levi Biel, *The Age of Feudalism.* San Diego: Lucent Books, 1994. A broad and easy-to-read overview of the political and social aspects of medieval times, including lords, serfs, vassals, manors, and knights.

Carole Lynn Corbin, *Knights.* New York: Franklin Watts, 1989. A brief, easy-to-read synopsis of medieval knights, castles, and chivalry.

Simon Goodenough, *The Renaissance.* London: Latimer House, 1979. A beautifully mounted and illustrated book that explores the main points of the European Renaissance, the last few centuries of the Middle Ages, in which learning, thinking, new inventions, explorations of new lands, and new scientific discoveries all contributed to sweeping changes that heralded the end of medieval society and the beginning of modern times.

Gertrude Hartman, *Medieval Days and Ways.* New York: Macmillan, 1960. A classic of its kind, this highly informative book covers nearly every aspect of medieval times, including a chapter on religious pilgrimages, in a straightforward and easy-to-read style. Highly recommended for all.

William W. Lace, *The Hundred Years' War.* San Diego: Lucent Books, 1994. This easy-to-read summary of the series of conflicts that raged between the English and French from 1337 to 1453 provides a broader context for understanding the political intrigues and bloody struggles that went on during the Middle Ages at the same time that pious pilgrims were traversing Europe in search of penance, salvation, and adventure.

Don Nardo, *The Roman Empire.* San Diego: Lucent Books, 1994. This concise overview of the last five centuries of Roman rule provides an entire chapter explaining the decay of the empire and how the so-called barbarian tribes eventually overran it, initiating the Middle Ages.

Jay Williams, *Life in the Middle Ages.* New York: Random House, 1966. A well-written and lively overview of medieval times with many colorful illustrations and reproductions of old paintings.

Jay Williams and Margaret B. Freeman, *Knights of the Crusades.* New York: American Heritage, 1962. A very well organized and informative volume that traces the upsurge of Christian zeal against the Muslims who had occupied the Holy Land and how European knights spent generations in an ultimately futile attempt to expel the non-Christians from Palestine. Contains many fine illustrations.

Works Consulted

John F. Benton, ed., *Self and Society in Medieval France: The Memoirs of Abbot Guibert of Nogent*. Translated by C .C. S. Bland. New York: Harper and Row, 1970. This autobiography of Abbot Guibert, who lived in northwestern France at the turn of the twelfth century, contains valuable and interesting information about that era, including monastic life, intellectual movements, the establishment of medieval towns, local beliefs and superstitions, and, of course, pilgrimages.

Geoffrey Chaucer, *The Canterbury Tales*. Translated by J. U. Nicolson. Vol. 22 of *Great Books of the Western World*. Chicago: Encyclopaedia Britannica, 1952. Written between 1387 and Chaucer's death in 1400, this ambitious work, composed of an 858-line prologue that introduces the characters and the 23 tales they tell, constitutes the most vivid and memorable surviving portrait of the members of a medieval pilgrimage. The work is also important because it reveals numerous facets of everyday life and thinking during the Middle Ages. Highly recommended, but because the text contains so many words, phrases, and references no longer common or familiar, it is advisable to consult a modern synopsis/analysis of the *Tales* before or while reading them.

Louise Collis, *Memoirs of a Medieval Woman: The Life and Times of Margery Kempe*. New York: Harper and Row, 1964. An informative and absorbing chronicle of an Englishwoman who lived in the late 1300s and early 1400s. Unable to read, she had the Bible read to her and became a religious fanatic. The long passages in which she goes on pilgrimages to Rome, Compostela, and Jerusalem and, because of her fanatical devotion to God, drives her traveling companions nearly crazy, are fascinating.

Anne Fremantle, *Age of Faith*. New York: Time, Inc., 1965. A very informative, well-written summary of the role played by the Christian Church in the Middle Ages. The discussion of the monastic religious orders is especially good. Many appropriate photos and reproductions of medieval art round out this fine volume.

Joseph Gies and Frances Gies, *Life in a Medieval City*. New York: Harper and Row, 1969. A well-organized and well-researched volume, broken down into sections such as "A Medieval Housewife," "Weddings and Funerals," "The Doctor," "Schools and Scholars," and "Town Government."

William Manchester, *A World Lit Only by Fire: The Medieval Mind and the Renaissance*. Boston: Little, Brown, 1992. Another thoughtful and riveting book by one of the most renowned and also one of the best modern historians (author also of the widely read *American Caesar*). From his insightful opening, in which he explains the transition from the crumbling Roman Empire to the medieval kingdoms, to his epic telling of Magellan's round-the-world voyage, which forever changed Europe's view of its place in the world and in nature, Manchester traces the evolution of ideas throughout the turbulent centuries of the Middle Ages.

Dorothy Mills, *The Middle Ages*. New York: G. P. Putnam's Sons, 1935. This old but hardly dated volume by a noted scholar covers the whole pageant of medieval times. Includes ample commentary, many primary source quotations, and a chapter on travelers, including religious pilgrims. Highly recommended.

Eileen Power, *Medieval People*. New York: Barnes and Noble, 1963. The author devotes an entire chapter to each of six real people who lived in medieval times, explaining how they lived and what they thought about their neighbors, the world, and God. The section on Madame Eglentyne, the real-life prioress of Chaucer's *Canterbury Tales*, is especially good.

Edith Rickert et al., eds., *Chaucer's World*. New York: Columbia University Press, 1948. An excellent collection of actual documents from the Middle Ages, including reports of monarchs' and other pilgrims' visiting shrines, a description of a knight visiting the pope, the itinerary of a trip from London to Rome, graphic accounts of famines and the Black Death, and a list of the contents of a nobleman's country manor.

Marjorie Rowling, *Life in Medieval Times*. New York: Berkley Publishing, 1968. This very well written overview of medieval life contains a great deal of information about religious pilgrimages, as well as about the way a country manor ran, what life was like inside the walls of a monastery, and how women were treated by their husbands and others.

Merle Severy, ed., *The Age of Chivalry*. Washington, DC: National Geographic Society, 1969. A magnificent volume that covers the Middle Ages in a series of excellent essays, each by a noted scholar, with titles such as "The World of Charlemagne," "Tracing William the Conqueror," and "The World of Richard the Lionheart." Contains a long, detailed examination of the towns and shrines along the route to Santiago de Compostela in Spain, one of the major attractions for medieval pilgrims, as well as plenty of information on monks, monasteries, and cathedrals. All sections are highlighted by numerous appropriate and often stunning photographs and reproductions. Very highly recommended.

Hugh Trevor-Roper, *The Rise of Christian Europe*. New York: Harcourt, Brace, and World, 1965. This well-written and interesting study by a noted historian traces the course of medieval civilization from the fall of Rome, through the so-called Dark Ages, the Crusades, and the Renaissance.

Charles Van Doren, *A History of Knowledge: Past, Present, and Future*. New York: Ballantine Books, 1991. Van Doren's colorful and flowing prose illuminates this excellent study of the evolution of Western thought. His discussions of the meaning and importance of Augustine's *The City of God*, the subsequent "obsession" with God of medieval people, and the "noble experiment" constituted by the church's attempt to establish a theocracy in Europe are first-rate scholarship and riveting reading.

Clara Winston and Richard Winston, *Daily Life in the Middle Ages*. New York: American Heritage, 1975. A fine overview of medieval times, including, in addition to discussions of lords, serfs, manors, friars, and the like, information about sites and relics visited by religious pilgrims, hospices for pilgrims, and swindlers who preyed upon these travelers along the way.

Additional Works Consulted

Frederick B. Artz, *The Mind of the Middle Ages, A.D. 200–1500: An Historical Survey*. New York: Knopf, 1954.

J. J. Bagley, *Life in Medieval England*. New York: G. P. Putnam's Sons, 1960.

H. S. Bennett, *Life on the English Manor: A Study of Peasant Conditions, 1150–1400*. Cambridge, England: Cambridge University Press, 1960.

P. Boissonnade, *Life and Work in Medieval Europe*. Translated by Eileen Power. New York: Knopf, 1927.

Norman F. Cantor, ed., *The Medieval World: 300–1300*. New York: Macmillan, 1963.

Ernst R. Curtius, *European Literature and the Latin Middle Ages*. Translated by Willard R. Trask. New York: Pantheon, 1953.

William S. Davis, *Life on a Medieval Barony*. New York: Harper and Row, 1951.

Norton Downs, ed., *Basic Documents in Medieval History*. Princeton, NJ: D. Van Nostrand, 1959.

Robert B. Downs, *Books That Changed the World*. New York: Penguin, 1983.

Margaret Drabble, ed., *The Oxford Companion to English Literature*. Oxford: Oxford University Press, 1985.

Georges Duby, ed., *The Knight, the Lady, and the Priest: The Making of Modern Marriage in Medieval France*. New York: Pantheon, 1983.

————, "Revelations of the Medieval World," in *A History of Private Life*, Vol. 2. Cambridge, MA: Harvard University Press, 1988.

Otto Friedrich, *The End of the World: A History*. New York: Fromm International, 1986.

V. H. H. Green, *Medieval Civilization in Western Europe*. New York: St. Martin's Press, 1971.

Graham Hancock, *The Sign and the Seal: The Quest for the Lost Ark of the Covenant*. New York: Simon and Schuster, 1992.

James Harpur and Jennifer Westwood, *The Atlas of Legendary Places*. New York: Weidenfeld and Nicolson, 1989.

Edward T. McLaughlin, *Studies in Medieval Life and Literature*. Freeport, NY: Books for the Libraries Press, 1972.

Karl F. Morrison, *Europe's Middle Ages: 565–1500*. Glenview, IL: Scott, Foresman, 1970.

Henri Pirenne, *Medieval Cities: Their Origins and the Revival of Trade*. New York: Doubleday, 1956.

Eileen Power, *Medieval Women*. Cambridge, England: Cambridge University Press, 1975.

Pat Rogers, ed., *The Oxford Illustrated History of English Literature*. Oxford: Oxford University Press, 1987.

Richard Tarnas, *The Passion of the Western Mind: Understanding the Ideas That Have Shaped Our World View*. New York: Ballantine Books, 1991.

Barbara W. Tuchman, *A Distant Mirror: The Calamitous 14th Century*. New York: Knopf, 1978.

Index

Adam of Usk, 37
Adams, Henry, 62
Aelfric the Grammarian, 20
Alps, crossing of, 8, 66-67
Assisi, Italy, 57
  basilica of St. Francis at,
    76-77
Augustine, Saint, of Hippo,
  15, 22

Battle of Tours, 17
Beckett, Thomas, 24-25
Benedict of Nursia, Saint,
  21, 30
Bernard of Saint Michael's
  Mount, 65
Bethlehem, 75, 78
Betson, Thomas, 31
Black Death, 48-50
  as God's wrath, 50-52
  death toll of, 49
Boccaccio, Giovanni, 49
bubonic plague. *See* Black
  Death

Calvary, 74
camino francés (French
  pilgrimage road), 61, 76
The Canterbury Tales
  (Chaucer), 23-26, 28-30,
  33, 53
cathedral of Saint James at
  Santiago de Compostela,
  61
Charlemagne, 18, 54
Charles VI (king of France),
  48
Chaucer, Geoffrey, 23-25
Chauliac, Guy de, 49-50
Christianity, 18, 79

City of God (Augustine), 15
civitas Dei (city of God), 15
civitas terrena (earthly city),
  15
clergy
  hierarchy of, 21
  rivalry among, 26-27
Colloquium (Aelfric), 20
Compostela, Santiago de,
  57, 63, 76
  cathedral of, 61
cross of Christ. *See* true
  cross

D'Anglure, Seigneur, 73
Decameron (Boccaccio),
  49-50
*Description of the Holy
Land* (Poloner), 72-73
Dome of the Rock, 68, 78
Dominic Saint, 27, 57
Dominican order, 27

Edward, Saint, Shrine of, 8
Eglentyne, Madame
  (Chaycer's prioress), 30
erysipelas, 48

fealty (loyalty), 17
feudal system, 16-20
Flagellants, 51
Francis of Assisi, Saint, 27,
  57, 79
Franciscan order, 27, 57
friars, 27
Fulk of Anjou, 32, 65

Georges, Père, 76
Gildas (Welsh chronicler),
  13

God, obsession with, 9-10
Goths, 15
Gower, John, 28
Guibert of Nogent, 22,
  46-47, 64, 65
Guilleville, Guillaume de,
  52
Guzman, Domingo de. *See*
  Dominic, Saint

Henry II (king of England),
  24
Hepatitis, 46
Higden, Ranulf, 8
highwaymen, 46-47
Holy Land, 22, 65
Holy Sepulchre, 73, 78
Holy Vernicle, 60
homage, ceremony of, 17
hospices, 39-40, 71
hostels, 41
Itineraries (Wey), 68-69

Jaffa (city in Palestine), 68,
  69, 70-71
James, Saint, 61, 63
Jerome, Saint, 75
Jerusalem, 57, 71-77
  Count Fulk's pilgrimage
    to, 32, 65
  divine summons to, 22
  modern pilgrimages to,
    77-78
Judas Iscariot, 59

Kempe, Margery, 30-32, 36,
  42, 56, 57, 66, 74

Langland, William, 36
language manuals, 41

leprosy, 48
lodgings, 39-41

manor (country estate), 16
manorial system, 19
Martel, Charles, 19
medieval, definition of, 11
Middle Ages
    cultural influence of
        ancient Rome, 13-15
    feudal system, 16-17,
        19-20
    life in, 11-12
    supremacy of Church
        during, 20-21
miracles
    at Compostela, 63-64
    at Saint Germer's Abbey,
        57
    of Holy Vernicle, 60
    of Saint Dominic, 57
Mirour de l'omme (Gower),
    28
Miscellaneous Inquisition,
    16
monastic orders, 21
monks, 21, 27
    relationship with friars
        and priests, 26
Mont-Saint-Michel, 62
Muhammad, 78
Muslims, 69, 75, 78
    defeat at Battle of Tours,
        17

Nazareth, 78
nuns, 28-29

"On the Government of
    God" (Salvian), 14

Palestine, 65
Paston, Margaret, 32
Paul the Deacon, 13

Peter, Saint, 59-60, 70
    basilica of, 59, 76
Petrarch, 49
pilgrimages
    by proxy, 38
    difficulties of, 43-52
    goals of, 53
    in modern times, 76-79
    lodging during, 39-41
    motives for, 23, 32, 65
    preparation for, 34-36
pirates, 46-47
Poloner, John, 72
pope, and worldly power, 20
Poynings, Richard, 55
priesthood, 21
priests, 21
    monks and, mutual
        contempt of, 26-27

relics, 53-56
Richard of Saint Vannes, 72
Richard II (king of
    England), 8
Rocamadour, (French
    pilgrimage site), 57
Roland (medieval French
    hero), 54, 57
Roman Empire, 11
    cultural leftovers of,
        13-15
    fall of, 12
Rome, 57, 58, 76
    sacked by Goths, 15
    shrines of, 59-61
Ronciere, Charles de la, 41

Saint Anthony's fire, 48
Saint Croix, Church of,
    54-55
Saint Augustine, 15, 22
Saint Benedict, 30
Saint Benedict of Nursia, 21
Saint Dominic, 27, 57

Saint Francis, 27, 57, 79
Saint Germer's Abbey, 57
Saint Leonard's Priory, 32
Saint James, 63
    cathedral of, 61, 63
Saint Jerome, 75
Saint Paul's Cathedral
    (London), 55
Saint Peter's Basilica
    (Rome), 59, 76
Saint Peter's Caves, 70
Salvian, 14
sanitation, 43-46
Saracens (Muslims), 69-73,
    75
Sea of Galilee, 78-79
sea travel, 44-46
    negotiating for, 67-68
shrines, 56-58
superstition, 11

Tafur, Pero, 8, 69, 75
The Tale of Beryn, 53
Tertullian, 11, 12, 13
theocracy, 20-21
tithe, 26
Travels (Tafur), 69
true cross, 53, 54, 55
vassals, 16
Venice, Italy, 66, 67
Veronica, Saint, 60
Vision of Piers the Plowman
    (Langland), 36

Walsingham (English
    pilgrimage site), 32
Weaver, William, 31, 66
Wey, William, 68-69
wife of Bath, 29-30
women
    as pilgrims, 30-31
    lowliness of, 31-32, 33

Picture Credits

Cover photo by Stock Montage, Inc.

The Bettmann Archive, 9, 17, 23, 24, 25, 36, 40, 44, 51 (bottom), 54 (both), 58, 60 (both), 66, 67, 72

Library of Congress, 49 (bottom), 52

North Wind Picture Archives, 12, 13, 15, 19, 21, 22

Picture Book of Devils, Demons, and Witchcraft, Dover Publications, 20, 51 (top)

Reuters/Bettmann, 78

Stock Montage, Inc., 10, 18, 26, 27, 35, 39, 45, 47, 70

UPI/Bettmann, 62, 63, 77

About the Author

Don Nardo is an award-winning author whose more than seventy books cover a wide range of topics, including science, health, and the environment. His main field, however, is history and in addition to this volume on medieval pilgrimages his historical studies include *Braving the New World, The Mexican-American War, The U.S. Presidency, The Battle of Marathon, The Age of Pericles, Life in Ancient Greece, Life in Ancient Rome, The Age of Augustus,* and *The Punic Wars,* as well as biographies of Franklin D. Roosevelt, Thomas Jefferson, Julius Caesar, Cleopatra, and many others. Mr. Nardo also dabbles periodically in orchestral composition, oil painting, screenwriting, and film directing. He lives with his wife Christine on Cape Cod, Massachusetts.